# Stephen Leacock

**ALSO IN THE**
**EXTRAORDINARY CANADIANS**
**SERIES:**

*Big Bear* by Rudy Wiebe

*Lord Beaverbrook* by David Adams Richards

*Norman Bethune* by Adrienne Clarkson

*Emily Carr* by Lewis DeSoto

*Tommy Douglas* by Vincent Lam

*Glenn Gould* by Mark Kingwell

*Louis-Hippolyte LaFontaine and Robert Baldwin*
by John Ralston Saul

*Wilfrid Laurier* by André Pratte

*René Lévesque* by Daniel Poliquin

*Nellie McClung* by Charlotte Gray

*Marshall McLuhan* by Douglas Coupland

*L.M. Montgomery* by Jane Urquhart

*Lester B. Pearson* by Andrew Cohen

*Mordecai Richler* by M.G. Vassanji

*Louis Riel and Gabriel Dumont* by Joseph Boyden

*Pierre Elliott Trudeau* by Nino Ricci

**SERIES EDITOR:**
John Ralston Saul

# Stephen Leacock
*by* MARGARET MACMILLAN

*With an Introduction by*
## John Ralston Saul
SERIES EDITOR

EXTRAORDINARY
CANADIANS

PENGUIN CANADA

Published by the Penguin Group

Penguin Group (Canada), 90 Eglinton Avenue East, Suite 700, Toronto,
Ontario, Canada M4P 2Y3 (a division of Pearson Canada Inc.)

Penguin Group (USA) Inc., 375 Hudson Street, New York, New York 10014, U.S.A.
Penguin Books Ltd, 80 Strand, London WC2R 0RL, England
Penguin Ireland, 25 St Stephen's Green, Dublin 2, Ireland
(a division of Penguin Books Ltd)
Penguin Group (Australia), 250 Camberwell Road, Camberwell, Victoria 3124, Australia
(a division of Pearson Australia Group Pty Ltd)
Penguin Books India Pvt Ltd, 11 Community Centre, Panchsheel Park,
New Delhi – 110 017, India
Penguin Group (NZ), 67 Apollo Drive, Rosedale, North Shore 0745, Auckland,
New Zealand (a division of Pearson New Zealand Ltd)
Penguin Books (South Africa) (Pty) Ltd, 24 Sturdee Avenue, Rosebank,
Johannesburg 2196, South Africa

Penguin Books Ltd, Registered Offices: 80 Strand, London WC2R 0RL, England

First published 2009

1 2 3 4 5 6 7 8 9 10 (RRD)

Copyright © Margaret MacMillan, 2009
Introduction copyright © John Ralston Saul, 2009

Author representation: Westwood Creative Artists
94 Harbord Street, Toronto, Ontario M5S 1G6

Manufactured in the U.S.A.

LIBRARY AND ARCHIVES CANADA CATALOGUING IN PUBLICATION

MacMillan, Margaret, 1943–
Stephen Leacock / Margaret MacMillan.

(Extraordinary Canadians)
ISBN 978-0-670-06681-0

1. Leacock, Stephen, 1869–1944.
2. Humorists, Canadian (English)—20th century—Biography.
3. Authors, Canadian (English)—20th century—Biography.
I. Title.  II. Series: Extraordinary Canadians

PS8523.E15Z882 2009      C818'.5209      C2009-900457-7

Visit the Penguin Group (Canada) website at **www.penguin.ca**

Special and corporate bulk purchase rates available; please see
**www.penguin.ca/corporatesales** or call 1-800-810-3104, ext. 477 or 474

This book was printed on 30% PCW recycled paper

## CONTENTS

# John Ralston Saul

How do civilizations imagine themselves? One way is for each of us to look at ourselves through our society's most remarkable figures. I'm not talking about hero worship or political iconography. That is a danger to be avoided at all costs. And yet people in every country do keep on going back to the most important people in their past.

This series of Extraordinary Canadians brings together rebels, reformers, martyrs, writers, painters, thinkers, political leaders. Why? What is it that makes them relevant to us so long after their deaths?

For one thing, their contributions are there before us, like the building blocks of our society. More important than that are their convictions and drive, their sense of what is right and wrong, their willingness to risk all, whether it be their lives, their reputations, or simply being wrong in public. Their ideas, their triumphs and failures, all of these somehow constitute a mirror of our society. We look at these people, all dead, and discover what we have been, but also what we can be. A mirror is an instrument for measuring ourselves. What we see can be both a warning and an encouragement.

These eighteen biographies of twenty key Canadians are centred on the meaning of each of their lives. Each of them is very different, but these are not randomly chosen great figures. Together they produce a grand sweep of the creation of modern Canada, from our first steps as a democracy in 1848 to our questioning of modernity late in the twentieth century.

All of them except one were highly visible on the cutting edge of their day while still in their twenties, thirties, and forties. They were young, driven, curious. An astonishing level of fresh energy surrounded them and still does. We in the twenty-first century talk endlessly of youth, but power today is often controlled by people who fear the sort of risks and innovations embraced by everyone in this series. A number of them were dead—hanged, infected on a battle-field, broken by their exertions—well before middle age. Others hung on into old age, often profoundly dissatisfied with themselves.

Each one of these people has changed you. In some cases you know this already. In others you will discover how through these portraits. They changed the way the world hears music, thinks of war, communicates. They changed how each of us sees what surrounds us, how minorities are treated, how we think of immigrants, how we look after each other, how we imagine ourselves through what are now our stories.

You will notice that many of them were people of the word. Not just the writers. Why? Because civilizations are built around many themes, but they require a shared public language. So Laurier, Bethune, Douglas, Riel, LaFontaine, McClung, Trudeau, Lévesque, Big Bear, even Carr and Gould, were masters of the power of language. Beaverbrook was one of the most powerful newspaper publishers of his day. Countries need action and laws and courage. But civilization is not a collection of prime ministers. Words, words, words—it is around these that civilizations create and imagine themselves.

The authors I have chosen for each subject are not the obvious experts. They are imaginative, questioning minds from among our leading writers and activists. They have, each one of them, a powerful connection to their subject. And in their own lives, each is engaged in building what Canada is now becoming.

That is why a documentary is being filmed around each subject. Images are yet another way to get at each subject and to understand their effect on us.

The one continuous, essential voice of biography since 1961 has been the *Dictionary of Canadian Biography.* But there has not been a project of book-length biographies such as Extraordinary Canadians in a hundred years, not since the Makers of Canada series. And yet every generation understands the past differently, and so sees in the mirror of these remarkable figures somewhat different lessons. As history rolls on, some truths remain the same while others are revealed in a new and unexpected way.

What strikes me again and again is just how dramatically ethical decisions figured in these people's lives. They form the backbone of history and memory. Some of them, Big Bear, for example, or Dumont, or even Lucy Maud Montgomery, thought of themselves as failures by the end of their lives. But the ethical cord that was strung taut through their work has now carried them on to a new meaning and even greater strength, long after their deaths.

Each of these stories is a revelation of the tough choices unusual people must make to find their way. And each of us as readers will find in the desperation of the Chinese revolution, the search for truth in fiction, the political and military dramas, different meanings that strike a personal chord. At first it is that personal emotive link to such figures which draws us in. Then we find they are a key that opens the whole society of their time to us. Then we realize that in that 150-year period many of them knew each other, were friends, opposed each other. Finally, when all these stories are put together, you will see that a whole new debate has been created around Canadian civilization and the shape of our continuous experiment.

Stephen Leacock seems at first a deeply contradictory figure—the funniest of men, who through ironic laughter brings each of us back to the deep truths in our character, yet also the deadly serious conservative economist who fights for a disappearing idea of empire. Perhaps that contradiction remains as true about Canada today as it once was about Leacock. Margaret MacMillan is a master of the imperial mind. She seeks out those places where individual character meets great events. Here she has released Leacock's humour into our contemporary psyche, so that we see through him how Canada remains as it has always been, a deeply ironic country.

# CHAPTER ONE

# Who Was Stephen Leacock and Why Should We Care?

In 1910 a young professor at McGill published a little book of comic sketches at his own expense. He already had a small reputation as a promising scholar; four years previously he had published a textbook on the relatively new discipline of political science. In the normal way of such things, this new book would have disappeared without a trace, a few copies surviving perhaps in someone's attic or a library or two. Its author, though, was Stephen Leacock and the book, *Literary Lapses,* contains some of the funniest pieces ever written in Canada. Even those who know nothing of his other work have read "My Financial Career" or seen the animated cartoon made by the National Film Board.

Leacock followed *Literary Lapses* a year later with *Nonsense Novels* and then in 1912 with perhaps his greatest work of all, *Sunshine Sketches of a Little Town.* He became an international star overnight. His pieces were published in Canadian newspapers and magazines, of course, but also in New York and London. Publishers begged him for his latest work. Theatre producers in London suggested he write plays. Charlie Chaplin asked him for a screenplay. A young F. Scott Fitzgerald wrote from Princeton to say how much his own writing was influenced by Leacock. Audiences paid handsomely to hear his lectures. When he arrived in England on a lecture tour in 1921, he had to hold a press conference.

In the days before radio and television, people still read out loud to one another in the evenings, and Leacock's work was meant to be heard. Indeed, he usually tried it out on his own circle before he published it. My own mother, who was a girl in England between the world wars, remembers the pleasure and anticipation of knowing there was another Leacock book out and that her uncles, who read so well, would be bringing it to a family evening. Like many people outside Canada, she knew of only a few Canadian writers: in her case, Mazo de la Roche, who wrote the wildly popular Jalna series, and Stephen Leacock.

Although he remained at McGill until he retired, much of Leacock's life was taken up with his writing and lecturing. He published almost one book of comic pieces a year until he died and frequently a more serious book as well. His death, in 1944, was national and international news. "We wish he could have stayed longer," said *The New York Times,* "but he had and gave the rest of us a good time." Three months later, the United States named one of its Liberty ships, designed to ferry material across the Atlantic, the SS *Stephen Leacock.*

While many of his most famous books have remained in print, Leacock's reputation, as so often happens with writers, dwindled after his death. His conservatism, his enthusiasm for the British Empire, his retrograde and public views on women, his belief that some races were superior to others—all made him out of step with the new, multi-ethnic Canada that was emerging in the second half of the twentieth century. His more serious books, on politics, history, and economics, are badly dated and appear to have little to say to the world of today. His beloved country house near Orillia, Ontario, has been preserved as a slightly fading museum, and a small band of Leacock devotees do their best to keep his memory alive. His name lingers on the Leacock Medal for Humour and, less happily, in the name of a Toronto high school where in 2006 police rounded up young Muslims alleged to be terrorists.

Yet we should remember him. His work reminds us of ourselves as we were, of a Canada of small towns and farms, and where, when people, especially English speakers, talked of Home they did not mean this country. Ambitious young people, like Leacock, longed for city life, but they never, again like Leacock, completely cut their ties to the country-side. Canada was a new country—only two years older than Leacock himself—and still trying to work out what sort of nation it was. (It has never really stopped.) Its wealth was still in its farms and forests, but the burgeoning numbers of mills and factories, the miles of railways, and the solid head offices that were rising in Montreal and Toronto hinted at the newer, more urbanized Canada that was to come.

Canadians themselves were predominantly of Aboriginal, British, or French stock. Immigrants from elsewhere, especially Asia or southern Europe, were not welcome. Most people had to be content with a high-school education; Leacock was in the minority who got to university, and the universities themselves were tiny in comparison with the massive institutions of today. There was scarcely a Canadian publishing industry and only a handful of periodicals. Leacock made fun of the conservatism and stodginess of Canadian society. He watched it as it changed.

I wanted to write this book partly because the Ontario I grew up in was still very much like the world Leacock describes in, for example, *Sunshine Sketches of a Little Town.*

Ontario, especially in the countryside and the smaller towns, remained very British and mostly white. My father's cousins, near London, had inherited their political allegiances just like the people in Leacock's imaginary Mariposa. People listened in on the party telephone line shared among several houses; it was not seen as nosiness but as simple curiosity. Many parts of the province were still dry, vestiges of the temperance movement at the start of the twentieth century which Leacock had so hated. As they did in Mariposa, though, people found ways around prohibition. Dutton, near London, where my father spent the summers in the 1920s and 1930s, was dry, but everyone, including the local police and the local judges, knew that its hotel had a beer parlour in the back. Indeed, the hotelkeeper gave money to the temperance advocates every time a vote came up on the grounds that his business would be hurt if he got competition.

Much of what Leacock satirized has vanished—but not all. That is one of the reasons his humour has endured. What he saw in us then, he would still see today. Our smug assurance, for example, that the Canadian way of doing things is the right way. Or the suspicion we have of people we cannot fit into any category. Canadians then called them eccentrics; we call them oddballs. We were suspicious then and still are of people who do too well. We raise our hands in pious horror when the successful slip on banana peels, but we secretly enjoy the spectacle.

We still laugh at the sorts of things Leacock laughed at. Pomposity and self-importance, for example. Some of Leacock's funniest work is on the hypocrites, often unconscious ones, who set out rules for the rest of humanity that they are not prepared to keep themselves. He hated pretension, whether in the shape of the university president who quotes Latin to disguise the vacuity of his ideas or the society ladies with their Dante Club which meets to discuss four lines of the poet over a lavish lunch. Leacock sent up Canadians, but he was also laughing at himself. Surely that is one of the marks then and now of Canadian humour, that it is self-deprecating. It is also low-key and apparently gentle, but there is often a real sting in it.

Leacock wrote too much and often too fast, but at his best he wrote a marvellous clear prose. How could you improve on the opening to "My Financial Career," with its repetition of the one keyword? "When I go into a bank I get rattled. The clerks rattle me; the wickets rattle me; the sight of the money rattles me; everything rattles me." Like that other great humorist, P.G. Wodehouse, Leacock knew how to choose the perfect adjective or image. The landlady, he says in "Boarding-House Geometry," is a parallelogram, "an oblong angular figure." In "The Awful Fate of Melpomenus Jones," the soul of his unfortunate hero escapes his body like "a hunted cat passing over a garden fence."

We should never see him, though, solely as a humorist. He never did and nor did his contemporaries. He used humour in his serious work and touched on serious subjects in his humour. Although Leacock's more serious writing is almost completely forgotten today, rousted out only by the graduate student in search of a thesis topic or the occasional intellectual historian, he was a public intellectual in a country which boasted few such figures. He tackled the big questions (many of them still relevant today) of his own times. What are the responsibilities of governments to their citizens? How should we educate our young? How can we build a just society? How do we deal with the threat of war? What is the best way to get out of a depression? And he dealt with the great changes taking place in his own lifetime as Canada's economy grew, its population expanded, and it became an independent nation. He worried about the balance between the provinces and the federal government. He saw dangers in politicians becoming too comfortable in office and too cozy with powerful interests. He tried to find a middle way, a Canadian way, between over-regulation of society and selfish individualism. As Canadians still are, he was both attracted and repelled by the United States. Does some of this sound familiar?

As a man, Leacock was clever, opinionated, irascible, kind, awkward, charming. He grew to be set in his ways, but his imagination knew no bounds. He loved fishing, thinking, and drinking, often at the same time. He was reserved with most people but deeply attached to those who were closest to him. He had much success and a considerable amount of tragedy in his life. His comic writing made thousands happy. He himself was a pessimist and a cynic about many things. We remember him, or ought to, for his comic masterpieces, but he was also a witness to and participant in the growth of Canada as a nation.

# CHAPTER TWO

# The Making of an English Gentleman in Canada

Like many Canadians, Stephen Leacock started life in another country. He was born in 1869 in a small town in England, the third of what were to be eleven children. His ill-matched and feckless parents came from the upper-middle classes, an important distinction in Victorian Britain. She was what was called at the time a lady and he a gentleman. Agnes Butler's father was an Anglican clergyman, and her family had the more distinguished connections; an uncle was headmaster of the well-known boys' school Marlborough College, and another was dean of Merton College in Oxford. The Leacocks had more money. An ancestor who had shipped out to Madeira as a cabin boy had made his fortune in the wine business, and his descendants had established themselves as country gentlemen on the Isle of Wight. Peter Leacock, Stephen's father, grew up with the tastes of his class but no useful training for a career.

The marriage took place in haste, but there was plenty of leisure for repentance. Agnes was twenty-one and Peter only seventeen when they ran away to London and were secretly married. In a memoir Agnes wrote near the end of her life, she expressed her sorrow and shame at deceiving her family but hinted that it was because Peter was a Roman Catholic and not yet of age. Their first son was born, though, a mere seven months after the hasty ceremony. Both families were furious with the young couple, and in 1867 they were shipped out to South Africa, where they were supposed to become farmers. Locusts, lack of experience, and their general lack of suitability for pioneer life on the land brought the couple back to England a year later. Peter Leacock's father, acting—so Stephen Leacock later facetiously remarked in his fragment of autobiography—on the principle that he wanted the Isle of Wight to himself, arranged to send his wayward son off to Kansas to try his hand at farming a second time. Agnes Leacock and her children, for there were now several, waited behind in cramped rented rooms for the summons to the Kansas farm. It never came. Instead Peter returned, a failure yet again. He and Agnes hung about, waiting to see what their elders would decree next.

As an adult, Stephen Leacock returned to Porchester in Hampshire, the only place he remembered from his early days in England. He found the house in which they had all lived. "I had no idea it could have been as poor as that!" His mother, hanging on to her shreds of gentility, had called a tiny room, "the size of a box," her drawing room and another equally small one her breakfast room. Leacock, who rarely spoke about his feelings, felt hurt and humiliated at the sight. "It is better not to go back to the place you came from. Leave your memory as it is."

He never really forgave his Leacock grandfather for not doing more for his parents. Late in his life, when some family property was settled up in England, Leacock refused to take any of the silver or jewellery. On the other hand, throughout his life he treasured a small fragment of wood his grandfather had given him, which came from the American frigate *Chesapeake,* famous for its battle with the British in the War of 1812. And he was always proud, in an offhand way, of the fact that on both sides his family had been long established in Hampshire, "not of course the real thing going back to the Conquest, but not bad."

In 1876, when Stephen was six years old, the Leacock family finally shipped out again, this time to a farm in Canada near Lake Simcoe. "Our farm was up in a lost corner of Ontario," Leacock wrote, "but the locality doesn't particularly matter. They're all the same from Ontario to Ohio." The bush had been cleared only within living memory and the roads were still primitive tracks. The nearest village, Sutton, is now increasingly a dormitory for Toronto, but in those days it was a tiny hamlet and it took a major expedition to get there or to the lake. "We lived in an isolation unknown in these days of radio, anywhere in the world," Leacock wrote in "My Remarkable Uncle," one of his finest pieces. "We were thirty-five miles from a railway. There were no newspapers. Nobody came and went. There was nowhere to come and go. In the solitude of the dark winter nights the stillness was that of eternity."

The local school was a mile away, and while the other boys walked barefoot in the warm weather, the Leacocks did not. It was, said Leacock, "a question of caste and thistles." Although the children were expected to do chores—Leacock remembered the early mornings clearing the manure out of the barns and plowing with a team of horses—the family were a cut above their neighbours. Leacock later made much of the poverty of his childhood, but there was always some money to cushion their lives. Agnes Leacock got sums of money from her family at irregular intervals and had her own income of $80 a month, which was what a high-school teacher was paid. There were always hired hands and domestic servants and, for at least a few summers, a rented house on the shore of Lake Simcoe.

Mrs. Leacock was determined that her children should remain part of the class into which they had been born, and that they should keep their English accents. She pulled them out of the local school and tried, with little success, to teach them at home. Eventually some money came from England and she was able to hire a private tutor. Leacock, who was, he said immodestly, the cleverest of the children as well as his mother's favourite, took off "like an arrow."

The farm itself was never a success, partly because Peter Leacock had little idea of how to manage it and partly because the Leacocks, with their usual luck, had arrived in Ontario when there was a slump in agricultural prices. The debts, the unpaid bills, and the weeds grew while Peter increasingly found comfort in drink. According to his son, he also lashed out at his wife and the two older boys. Agnes, whom Leacock revered all his life, tried with limited success to hide the state of things from her other children. "In fact," he wrote in his unfinished memoir, "the sight and memory of what domestic tyranny in an isolated, lonely home, beyond human help, can mean, helped to set me all the more firmly in the doctrine of the rights of man, and Jefferson's liberty."

In 1881 his father took off for the West, where fresh opportunities seemed to promise. He came back only briefly, as poor as before and still drinking. There is a Leacock family story that he threatened Agnes with a knife and that Stephen, by now eighteen years old, took a horsewhip to him and told him never to come back. Leacock in his memoir simply says his father left home for good and that it would be out of place to go into details. Father and son never met again. The senior Leacock bobbed up in Nova Scotia, living out his life as the well-respected and well-behaved "Captain Lewis," who, it was remarked, never took a drink.

The rest of the family were also abandoning the farm as they moved away first for schools and then into careers or marriage. Stephen Leacock was ruthlessly unsentimental in his memoir: "I at last got rid of the rotten old place on my mother's behalf simply by moving mother off it and letting it go to the devil." Yet his feelings about the country and his childhood were more complicated than that. "The 'stamp' I carry," he wrote in 1936, "is that of the farm in Georgina Township and my predilection is for the soil and the Canadian bush." He took pride in having survived life on the farm and having been toughened up by hard work.

As he admitted later in his life, the memories of the tougher side of life on the farm faded over the years and former farm boys like himself remembered only the space, the beauty of sunrises and sunsets, and the rhythms of the agricultural year. In *Arcadian Adventures with the Idle Rich,* the Wizard of Finance, a farmer who has apparently struck it rich when gold is discovered on his property, jettisons his fortune and flees the city. The gold strike turns out to be a chimera, and the Wizard stands happily with his son on his own hills: "they saw nothing but the land sloping to the lake and the creek murmuring again to the willows, while the off-shore wind rippled the rushes of the shallow water."

The city, with its possibilities and opportunities, beckoned Leacock as it did so many Canadians of his times, but he never completely turned his back on the country. In "Hidden Secrets of the City," a sketch he published in 1936, the narrator, at least partly based on Leacock himself, describes waiting to give a lecture on the current situation in Europe to a high-powered city audience. As he talks nervously to the president of a huge bank, both men discover that they come from farms. "Five minutes later, if the conversation of the great financier had been reported, it would have run like this—'You can do better with soy beans for hogs than you can in trying to raise grain for them.'" Most of the audience, it turns out, also started out on farms, and the narrator happily abandons his theme for the much more interesting ones of apple trees and early cucumbers.

Leacock knew that much of the nostalgia evinced by city people like himself was something of an affectation. In his loving reminiscences of his great friend Andrew Macphail, a fellow professor at McGill, he recalls Macphail's saying that there is nothing better than buttermilk (as he drank his whisky and soda) or lauding the taste of maple sap out of a wooden trough, "a beverage," says Leacock, "little better in reality than a solution of sawdust and dead flies." Leacock could have been talking of himself when he adds that behind the nostalgia, though, was "a deep-seated feeling that the real virtue of a nation is bred in the country, that the city is an unnatural product." Don't we still have that today with our enthusiasm for our cottages and for summer camps for our children?

Once Leacock could afford it, he bought property near where he had grown up and set out to be a part-time farmer. Being Leacock, he mocked the pretensions of the farm boys like himself who built themselves large country houses and believed they were coming home to the old farm. The vegetables he fussed over never made him money; indeed, quite the opposite. Ventures into such things as turkeys were even more expensive. His favourite niece, Barbara Nimmo, remembered a Thanksgiving turkey, the sole survivor of a flock of one hundred, which cost, if you calculated the total investment, $100 in pre–Second World War currency. "By well-designed capital expenditure, by drainage and by greater attention to detail," he wrote to a friend, he had managed to increase the deficit on his property enormously.

His early life on the farm, as Leacock often observed, had been marked by loneliness, but it also helped develop his imagination. He and his siblings had to make up their own amusements, whether it was exploring the bush or drawing pictures. Their only news came from the *London Illustrated News,* which tended to feature daring deeds and heroic battles. In the evenings their mother read to them, from Walter Scott (one of Leacock's heroes as a writer) or Mark Twain (another hero). In retrospect, Leacock always maintained that being read to was much better than watching a film. "We cannot have it both ways. Intensity of mental impression and frequency of mental impression cannot go together." Before he ever started to write, Leacock too learned how to tell stories to a listening audience.

The world of their geography lessons was a mysterious and exciting place. Africa's outline was there, but what lay in the interior still had to be mapped. The heart of the Arabian Peninsula was an uncharted desert. Great swaths of the North American West still remained to be surveyed and settled. Railways, telegraphs, and steamships were only starting to bring distant parts of the world into contact. In a late piece, written when he was nearly seventy, Leacock addressed the younger generation: "Your little world is shrunken, crowded—noisy and quarrelsome; it is like a street alley where once there was a silent wood." He preferred the silence of his youth, where he could imagine the great sailing ships, not the prosaic mechanical ones of the present, and where it was still possible to imagine being explorers in the trackless wastes or Robinson Crusoe or the Swiss Family Robinson on desert islands.

In 1882 Mrs. Leacock, who usually managed to find money when she needed it, sent Stephen to join his two older brothers as a boarder at Upper Canada College, the private Toronto school which had been educating young boys from good, or at least moneyed, families since 1829. Leacock stayed there for five years and ended up as head boy. Like the farm, Upper Canada College helped to form him and, like the farm, he remained ambivalent about it. Modelled on the great English private schools, it stressed classics over the sciences or history or languages as the basis of a good education. The great works in Latin and Greek, so it was assumed, were much superior to anything written since. Leacock, who was a good and bright student, liked the college and did well there, but he later wondered about the value of the education he received. "I acquired such a singular facility in handling Latin and Greek that I could take a page of either of them, distinguish which it was by merely glancing at it, and, with the help of a dictionary and a pair of compasses, whip off a translation of it in less than three hours." He never enjoyed it, he claimed, and was left with the sense that he had missed out on a proper appreciation of English literature and modern history, not to say mathematics. The pretentious humbug who covers up his ignorance by quoting Latin and Greek tags is a comic figure in Leacock's work just as he is in Shakespeare's.

Equally important, the college was supposed to turn unpolished Canadian boys into English gentlemen, something about which Leacock was later equally skeptical. "Slowly we learned the qualifications of a gentleman," he wrote in "The Struggle to Make Us Gentlemen," "and saw that the thing was hopeless." In one of his most moving pieces, "I'll Stay in Canada," he explains to an English audience that he simply would not fit in at "home." He was not really a gentleman. True, he could sound and act like one, but there were telling differences between him and English gentlemen. "I think we are a little too unrestrained and we have a way of referring to money, a thing of which you never definitely speak in England."

Leacock went on to the University of Toronto to study, not classics, but modern languages. He had an aptitude for languages and over time acquired a good half-dozen, from French to German and Russian. His mother was able to give him only a limited amount of help, and he lived meagrely, staying in unappetizing boarding houses where, he wrote, the boarders dined in dim basement rooms off beef "done up in some way after it was dead." This too, however, gave him material he could use later. One of his earliest and most famous pieces is "Boarding-House Geometry," which starts with the proposition that "All boarding houses are the same boarding house."

After a year of university, he was obliged to drop out to earn a living. As so many of his contemporaries did, he took a quick qualifying course to become a high-school teacher. His first job was in Uxbridge, Ontario, then a sleepy country town. He was a good teacher, Leacock says, but he was restless and unsatisfied. He felt that he was marking time, from what had not yet become clear, and that his education was unfinished. What he did know was that he did not want to settle down as a high-school teacher. Later, when he was a successful and contented teacher at McGill, he tried to explain why he had disliked high-school teaching so much. "The one means the boy; the other means the book." A neat aphorism which explains nothing, but then Leacock, who had the reserve of his times, never liked to examine his own heart too closely.

An offer to teach at his former school of Upper Canada College came as a partial reprieve. He could live comfortably on the promised salary of $700 per year and have enough spare time to resume his studies at the University of Toronto. He was able, not without difficulty, to persuade Uxbridge to release him. For the next ten years, from 1889 to 1899, Leacock combined teaching and studying. Although he graduated in modern languages in 1891, he started to study political economy on his own. (In those days the split between politics and economics was not as pronounced as it later became, and Leacock continued to do both until his retirement.) His colleagues and former students at Upper Canada remembered him as a congenial if rather lack-adaisical colleague. He taught well enough, although he knew he could have done better by his students: "They got nothing from me in the way of intellectual food but a lean and perfunctory banquet." He did his best to get out of the rest of his duties, such as escorting the boys to church.

Leacock later looked back on that period in his life with considerable bitterness: "I liked the last day of it as little as I liked the first." He resented what he saw as the lowly status of the schoolteacher and he feared, with some reason, that he was trapped in a job which gave him enough to get by on but which had few prospects. "Being appointed to the position of a teacher," he later wrote, "is like being hooked up through the braces and hung up against a wall. It is hard to get down again." In later life he could never resist taking a swipe at his first profession. Louis Riel, Leacock wrote in his 1941 history of Canada, divided his time between teaching and going partly crazy, "a thing quite intelligible to the profession." Leacock in those early years dreamed of escape but found it hard to save money, partly because he was obliged to help out his mother, who kept drifting into debt.

In fact, although he could not know it, he was laying the foundations of two successful careers, as a writer and an academic. He was developing new intellectual interests and learning how to write. He was also growing up, making friends, and falling in and out of love. He published his first sketches, made the decision to leave teaching for graduate study, and met the woman who would become his wife.

# CHAPTER THREE

# Escaping into Adulthood

Leacock made his escape (and that is how he saw it) from high-school teaching in 1899 when he enrolled in the Ph.D. program at the University of Chicago. He abandoned the study of languages, with few regrets, just as he had earlier given up on the classics, in favour of political science and economics. He had been reading on his own in the field for some years and may have already encountered the work of Chicago's most brilliant and original economist, Thorstein Veblen. Far more than the classics or languages, economics and its sister political science seemed to Leacock to be of immediate and contemporary relevance both for under-standing the world and in preparing the next generations to deal with it.

It is easy to see why he thought so. In his short lifetime, he had witnessed the effects on society of dramatic changes and fluctuations in the economy. His own family had been unable to weather the agricultural depression of the 1870s. His father and an uncle had moved west to make their fortunes in the Winnipeg boom of the 1880s and had both come home again when the bubble burst. He had seen the railways spreading across the continent and the steamships from around the world pouring into Canadian harbours to bring thousands of immigrants and to take away Canadian resources. Although agriculture remained the foundation of the Canadian economy, Canada was developing its own manufacturing sector. In 1900, although Leacock could not yet know it, the country was to enjoy the greatest and most prolonged economic boom in its short history. Big fortunes were being made and lost, but the benefits of prosperity were spread unequally throughout society. There was much to think about.

The University of Chicago was new (it was founded by the great robber baron John D. Rockefeller in 1891) and serious. Graduate students were expected to do sustained research in fields that would benefit society. As Leacock was to discover, there was little social life outside the classrooms. "Years and years later, when I visited Oxford," he wrote, "I realized this lack all over again with a sort of wistful jealousy and regret." The University of Chicago may have been dull, but it gave Leacock a solid education and his ticket to academic employment in the shape of his doctorate. It is not clear how much he learned of economics. Certainly in later years at McGill, there were many unkind remarks about his grasp of the subject and his lack of interest in keeping up to date. Perhaps he was not entirely joking when he later wrote, "The meaning of this degree is that the recipient of instruction is examined for the last time in his life, and is pronounced completely full. After this, no new ideas can be imparted to him."

In his reminiscences about his time in Chicago, Leacock is facetious about Veblen, whose lecturing style, he said, had "no manner, no voice, no art." He compliments Veblen for his deft turn of phrase but dismisses his work itself as laying the ground for behavioural economics, "which, I thank God, I am too old to learn." Yet if Leacock did not take away much from Veblen to use in his own classes, he was undoubtedly influenced by Veblen's insights into the nature of capitalism. In what is perhaps his most famous book, *The Theory of the Leisure Class,* published the year Leacock started in Chicago, Veblen argues that people accumulate wealth in part to emulate and to compete with others socially. The rich use their wealth to impress others in conspicuous consumption, including the conspicuous display of leisure. In the 1890s the opportunities for pursuing wealth were greater in North America than ever before and that in itself put a strain on society. Christian values (and North

Americans were largely churchgoers) and virtues such as thrift and caution which had been valued in a predominantly agricultural society no longer seemed to be rewarded while self-seeking and ruthless behaviour like that of the robber barons was. It is difficult in changing times, said Veblen, to know whether particular actions or people are praiseworthy or criminal.

Leacock, like Veblen, was well aware of the clash between the professed religious and ethical values of his own society and the new capitalism. Conservative by temperament, Leacock also strongly disliked the changes and the new rich they produced. In one of his serious books, *The Unsolved Riddle of Social Justice*, published in 1920, he inveighs against "the obvious and glaring fact of the money power, the shameless luxury of the rich, the crude, uncultivated and boorish mob of vulgar men and over-dressed women, that masqueraded as high society." It is largely in his comic writings, though, that he targets the shallow and pretentious rich. In one of his early sketches, "Old Junk and New Money," the Hespeler-Hyphen-Joneses collect pieces of rubbish which they insist are valuable antiques. An expensive clock does not work: "If it's a genuine Salvolatile, it won't go." They know a splendid man who can break anything for them and they have found a wonderful source for antiques in Holland: "It's just the dearest little place, nothing but little, wee, smelly shops filled with the most delightful things—all antique, everything broken." In "Life in the Open," the hostess talks about how she and her husband love the simple life in the country. "We're both so passionately fond of the open air. Ransome, will you close that window? There's a draught."

Although he was proud of his own family origins, Leacock also attacked snobbery. The Victorians, he says, for all their advances failed to get rid of the respect for status and privilege which scarred their society. The pointless English anecdote, he writes in "Humour as I See It," is like the following:

> His Grace the Fourth Duke of Marlborough was noted for the openhanded hospitality which reigned at Blenheim, the family seat, during his regime. One day on going in to luncheon it was discovered that there were thirty guests present, whereas the table only held covers for twenty-one. 'Oh, well,' said the Duke, not a whit abashed, 'some of us will have to eat standing up.' Everybody, of course, roared with laughter.

"My only wonder," said Leacock sourly, "is that they didn't kill themselves with it."

In *Arcadian Adventures with the Idle Rich*, second only to *Sunshine Sketches* as a sustained satire of a small society, Leacock targets not the small town but the world of the rich in a big city. On the gracious Plutoria Avenue, expensive cars move slowly along, bearing their passengers to the Mausoleum Club while birds, "the most expensive kind," sing in the trees. Children are wheeled out to enjoy the sun, which always seems to shine. "A million dollars of preferred stock laughs merrily in recognition of a majority control going past in a go-cart drawn by an imported nurse." If you were to climb to the roof of the Mausoleum Club you could see the slums in the distance. "But why should you?"

The rich manage to ignore both uncomfortable sights and thoughts. When a new, fire-breathing minister takes over St. Osoph's Presbyterian Church and tells his congregation that most of them are going to Hell, they do not take it personally at all. Rather they find it delightfully bracing and his audience grows by the week. The only problem is that the congregation—and the offerings—in the Anglican church, St. Asaph's, dwindle, and that worries the businessmen who have underwritten it. Fortunately their business experience comes to the rescue. "We have here practically the same situation," says one, "as we had with the two rum distilleries,—the output is too large for the demand." There is a solution to hand. "We'll propose a merger." Just like Standard Oil. Both men laughed: "One could hardly compare a mere church to a thing of the magnitude and importance of the Standard Oil Company."

A lawyer experienced in mergers advises the trustees of the two churches to create a new corporation on sound business lines. The minor issue of doctrines is easily settled: such things as creation or salvation of the soul will be dealt with by votes of the shareholders. "These," says the lawyer, "are not matters of first importance, especially as compared with the intricate financial questions which we have already settled in a satisfactory manner." Peace returns to Plutoria Avenue and its two churches. "Their bells call softly back and forward to one another on Sunday mornings and such is the harmony between them that even the episcopal rooks on the elm trees of St. Asaph's and the presbyterian crows in the spruce trees of St. Osoph's are known to exchange perches on alternate Sundays."

Leacock made fun of the rich, but he also liked the way they lived. "I like to mix with millionaires," he joked. "I like the things they mix." He himself was always conscious of the benefits of money. He had to take care of his family; he liked to live comfortably; and, as he prepared to go off to the University of Chicago, he met Beatrix Hamilton, the woman who would become his wife in 1900. Leacock had been in love before, once with a neighbour at Lake Simcoe who, when he proposed, had told him not to be ridiculous, that neither of them had any money. He also used to regale his friends with a story of how he followed a young woman to Colorado, where she was being treated for tuberculosis. While he waited at the foot of a mountain, she was in a sanatorium at the top. He was finally allowed to join her and her mother for an evening of hymn-singing. He, so he claimed, left the next day for home.

Beatrix Hamilton was the sort of woman Leacock liked. She was attractive, vivacious, and sporty. Moreover she came from a good family—her father was colonel of a well-known Toronto regiment, the Queen's Own Rifles, and her uncle was the great financier Sir Henry Pellatt, who was to squander much of his fortune a decade later in building his huge mansion, Casa Loma. Unusually for someone of her class, Beatrix had gone on the stage and had enjoyed a moderately successful career by the time she met Leacock. Indeed, they were married in New York, where she was then acting. She gave up her career to become Mrs. Stephen

Leacock, an increasingly demanding role as the years went by and Leacock became more successful.

Leacock had firm views on the place of women—in the home—and on their duties—marriage and children. He had no sympathy for the early Canadian feminists such as Nellie McClung, who had started campaigning for women's rights before the First World War. In "Truthful Oratory," one of his earlier comic pieces, he described what a male politician talking to a women's suffrage society would *really* like to say to them. "My own earnest, heartfelt conviction is that you are a pack of cats," the speech would start, and the speaker would describe his own ideal woman, "who can cook, mend clothes, talk when I want her to, and give me the kind of admiration to which I am accustomed." In his 1916 essay "The Woman Question," which was probably written in direct response to Nellie McClung's campaign for votes for women, he laughs at the pretensions of a group of women, "Superior Beings," who believe that when women have the vote the world will be a better place. In addition, and it was a point Leacock made frequently, women are simply not fitted to do men's work. A woman is not strong enough, he claimed, to lay bricks or dig coal, and as for business, she simply doesn't have the head. "Figures confuse her. She lacks sustained attention and in point of morals the average woman is, even for business, too crooked."

Of course, it is Leacock having fun, but he returns to the topic too often for it to be just that. In his dystopian and distinctly gloomy story "The Man in Asbestos: An Allegory of the Future," the narrator is horrified by the results of the emancipation of women: "Asbestos, do you think that those jelly-bag Equalities out on the street there, with their ash-barrel suits, can be compared for one moment with your unredeemed, unreformed, heaven-created, hobble-skirted women of the twentieth century?" Leacock deplored women competing with men in sports or anywhere else. "Look at any golf-links of today," he wrote in the 1930s, "the bright autumn landscape and the pleasant greens all spoiled by a bunch of tubby-looking women, all over the place."

To be fair, Leacock in his views on women, as in much else, was inconsistent. He could make sweeping generalizations about women and why they should not be emancipated, yet when it came to the individual women whom he knew and loved, he behaved quite differently. He had great respect, for example, for his sister Rosamond, whom he helped financially to become one of the first women doctors in Canada. (She later became a distinguished pathologist in Calgary.) He also encouraged, and indeed paid for, his beloved niece Barbara to go to university for both a bachelor's degree and a master's. He was capable too, as most of us are, of changing his mind as times changed. In "Woman's Level," one of his last pieces, published posthumously in 1945, he says that rights for women is a dead issue: "In the new world we are to make after the war, it must be taken for granted that women are to have all the political rights and professional rights that men have—the right to vote on anything and sit on anything that a man can sit on, a size larger if need be."

In his own marriage, he followed the prevailing pattern of his era. Although Beatrix Leacock was unusual for young women of her class in having had a career before she married—and on the stage moreover—she gave up her professional acting once she married and settled into the more conventional role of wife. The Leacock marriage seems to have been a very happy one, although the two lived what by today's standards might seem separate lives. Leacock had his club, his male friends, and his work, and his wife had her own social round. She was usually, though, the first audience for his writing and helped him with the editing of his books. Unfortunately no letters between the two appear to have survived and so it is difficult to gauge the strength of their feelings toward each other. Leacock himself never wrote about his marriage, although he occasionally hinted at the desolation he felt when his wife died.

In his reticence, he was very much a product of his place and times. Like many Victorians, he was not comfortable with writing about personal matters or emotions. When he writes about love, he almost always treats it as a joke or a mistake. He was contemptuous of the new writers such as James Joyce who tried to delve into human nature. Psychology, he said in his 1939 book, *Too Much College,* was a useless, and indeed dangerous, subject. "Plain right and wrong, common sense, goodness and badness get mixed up in a world that has a terrifying aspect of dark forces working through the individual and not of him."

One of Leacock's great models as a writer was Charles Dickens, but only the Dickens who created sunny characters, not the Dickens of Fagin and Bill Sykes. In an admiring biography he published in 1933, Leacock concentrates on such works as *Pickwick Papers,* and Dickens's great comic characters such as Mr. Micawber. He does not like gloomier later novels such as *Bleak House.* Paul Dombey, the poor little rich boy, whose death Dickens treats so movingly in *Dombey and Son,* is, for Leacock, a waste of Dickens's talent. "Sorrow as a deliberate luxury is a doubtful pursuit, a dubious form of art." We may ask why, says Robertson

Davies, the great Canadian novelist and literary critic, who has written with such insight about Leacock. "Did Leacock," Davies asks, "dislike the melancholy in Dickens because he feared its echo in himself?"

As a writer, Leacock often played the role of the simple, down-to-earth fellow who cannot abide highfalutin stuff that probes too deeply into the human condition. In his 1923 collection, *Over the Footlights,* he mocks the Russian novelists who deal with the dark side of life and parodies a translation of the great Norwegian playwright Henrik Ibsen, "Done out of the original Norwegian with an axe." He dismisses Greek tragedies as too lofty and sublime for the likes of him and is equally hostile to what he calls the modern Piffle Play, always, he says, "terribly perplexed, and with sixty per cent of sex in it." Give him, he says, the good old-fashioned melodramas. His parodies are not in the least funny because Leacock has no feeling for the originals. You do wonder, though, why he is so vehement in disliking them.

His favourite niece, Barbara Nimmo, said of him: "There was a certain shyness in his character—not completely sure about himself—an inadequacy about expressing his feelings towards people." When he received an offer in the 1930s from an English publisher to write his autobiography, he replied firmly, "I will only write it in my own way; nearly all reflections, very little life—and no personalia about people I have met...." Any discussion of sex made him particularly uncomfortable. In his serious, and deadly dull, book *Humour: Its Theory and Technique,* published in 1935, he grumbles about "the terrible obsession with sex which is creeping like a green slime all over our imaginative literature." He worried too that what he called that "sex stuff" was corroding "good wholesome humour."

The Leacocks started out their married life in Chicago, but increasingly they gravitated toward Montreal, where Stephen was offered a part-time teaching post at McGill in 1901. When he got his doctorate in 1903, he at once became a full-time lecturer. In 1908 he was made a full professor and became chair of the Department of Economics and Political Science, and there he remained until 1936.

At the same time, Leacock started on his career as a writer. In his first years at McGill, he worked on *Elements of Political Science,* a textbook for undergraduates, which he published in 1906. It was an immediate success and remained in print for years. Leacock made more money from it than any other of his books. He followed it up with a second serious book for the Makers of Canada series, *Baldwin, Lafontaine, Hincks: Responsible Government.* He was also becoming known as an entertaining and stimulating lecturer. In 1906 his lectures on the British Empire caught the attention of Earl Grey, the Governor General, who arranged for him to go on an extended lecture tour in 1907–08 of Great Britain, South Africa, New Zealand, and Australia. His career as an academic was well and successfully launched.

In 1910, however, he took the step that was to make him an internationally known writer when he decided to make a little book out of some of the comic sketches he had published here and there over the years. His wife and a friend managed to track most of them down (they included pieces such as "My Financial Career" and "Boarding-House Geometry"), and Leacock sent off a manuscript to the American publisher Houghton Mifflin. The rejection letter that came back said that humour was too "uncertain." One of his closest friends advised him to let the matter lie; publishing light stuff would hurt his reputation as an up-and-coming academic.

By a lucky chance Leacock's brother George read through the manuscript one evening. "Oh, hell! These are good," he said. "Steve, why don't you just publish these yourself?" Leacock accepted the dare and found a Montreal publisher who agreed to undertake the work for a guarantee of the costs of some $500. The amount sounds small, but at a time when his annual salary was around $2,500 a year, he was taking a considerable gamble. The first printing of 3,000 copies of *Literary Lapses* sold out quickly and Leacock made a decent profit of $230. Even more fortunately, a visiting English publisher, John Lane from the firm of Bodley Head, picked up one of the copies to read on the trip back to England. Once there he cabled Leacock an offer which Leacock enthusiastically accepted, not however without showing a scrupulous attention to details which was to mark all his dealings with publishers.

*Literary Lapses* came out in Britain and then in the United States, and it was followed in 1911 by another collection, *Nonsense Novels*. Leacock's first reviews were what every young writer dreams of. *Literary Lapses* was "charming and humorous," "exceedingly clever and original," a "treasure." Leacock was compared to Lewis Carroll or Mark Twain. "Genuine gold on every page," said *Punch* of *Nonsense Novels*. "Mr. Leacock is the best jester lately imported from the other side of the Atlantic," said the London *Evening News*. "The greatest humorist of the age" was the view of A.P. Herbert, himself a very funny writer. Theodore Roosevelt, the American president, paid Leacock the compliment of quoting his phrase about "riding madly off in all directions" in a speech. It was an image that might have done for Leacock himself as he increasingly juggled his careers as an academic, a public intellectual, a serious writer, and a humorist.

# Riding Madly Off in All Directions

As Leacock settled into maturity, he was a handsome, burly man, with a shock of hair and luxuriant moustache, and a ruddy complexion, like someone who had spent a lot of his time out of doors. His eyes were blue—or were they hazel? One niece believed that their colour changed with his mood. Although he spent a lot on his clothes and got at least two new suits a year from his tailor, he was dishevelled, like a bear, said one friend, that had been taught to dress itself but "had never got it right." His hats looked like they had been run over. His raccoon coat with its missing buttons and bits falling off was famous around McGill; students believed that it went back to the time of the Riel Rebellion. If Leacock could not find what he needed, he would simply grab whatever came to hand, a tie to hold up his trousers or a safety pin to attach his house key to his watch chain. In the summers he wandered around his beloved property near Orillia in trousers that were always white at the start of the season and black by the end. Occasionally strangers mistook him for a tramp.

"His was the carelessness of a locomotive engineer," argued one of his closest friends, "who knows that he has a big job to do and gives it all his attention, and doesn't have to bother about clothes to keep up his social position." Certainly when it came to his work, Leacock was highly disciplined in his habits. He wrote every morning for several hours. He did not usually find it necessary to edit his own work and he seldom rewrote anything. Indeed he often did not bother to look at his proofs. Was it self-confidence or indifference? Robertson Davies believed it was vanity, that Leacock felt that he had mastered everything he needed to know about writing. In one of his last books, *How to Write,* Leacock laid out the rules, as he saw them, for young writers. He had, he told them, learned how to use material from his own life: "I can write up anything now at a hundred yards." It is really quite simple, he tells his readers: "Writing comes from having something to say and trying hard to say it." He himself, he boasts, has done very well financially from doing just that.

Once Leacock had sent a book off to a publisher, he immediately got down to writing the next one. His output was extraordinary. He could write a short story in an hour or two, often because he had already tried it out on an audience. "I can hit 3,500 words to the syllable," he once said, "knowing it beforehand...." His work appeared everywhere, in the most important and popular newspapers and magazines on both sides of the Atlantic. When he could, he would read out what he had been writing to whoever was handy. If it was something funny, he would often have to stop while he laughed at his own jokes. Leacock never wasted anything. He worked, he said, on the same principle as the lemonade maker who squeezes out the lemons at the bottom of the empty jug to make another round. Lectures became articles, and articles became collections in a book. In his lifetime he published more than sixty books, of humour of course but also on the British Empire, education, economics, Canadian history, American history, as well as biographies of his great literary heroes Charles Dickens and Mark Twain.

Leacock did well out of his writing. In particularly good years in the 1920s, for example, he made $40,000—that at a time when his salary from McGill was around $5,500 and a university president's annual salary was around $18,000, and when he was able to build his nineteen-room country house at Old Brewery Bay for $17,000. He was very conscious that he was writing for money. His letters to his publishers are full of queries about royalties or complaints that they are not doing enough to promote his books. "<u>Do Rush the book &</u> <u>boom it</u>," he urged a Toronto publisher in 1930. With a most un-Canadian lack of modesty, he often wrote his own glowing notices for the publishers. Stephen Leacock is known around the world, he said in the copy for *My Remarkable Uncle,* and here he shows his "extraordinary power" again.

At times his haste and his lack of editing showed. Too many of his books have unnecessary information that he could not bear to waste. In his history of Montreal, for example, there is a long disquisition on how to build a bridge. He also cut corners. He reused the same passage about the dullness of life on the farm in *My Discovery of the West,* "My Remarkable Uncle," and *Canada.* And he could simply be dull. Carl Goldenberg, who had been one of his students and later had a distinguished political career, once let Leacock know that an article for an American magazine was not all that good. "Look," said Leacock, "all I have to do is put a pen between two toes and I'll be paid $500 for what results therefrom."

His growing affluence made it possible for the Leacocks to live in considerable style with several servants and what was at the time the luxury of an automobile. In 1909 he and his wife moved into a large rented house, which they later bought, on the Côte-des-Neiges near McGill. The University Club, which he helped found, became a home away from home. Leacock usually dropped in after his classes for a drink and to play billiards with his greatest friend at McGill, René du Roure, the small, elegant Frenchman who was head of the French department. Both men played badly, but Leacock usually won because he kept up a steady flow of comments as du Roure was about to take his shot. If Leacock was in a mood to tell stories, a crowd would gather around his favourite leather armchair and people would call their friends to come down. Leacock loved to hold forth, but he was not good at listening to others. A number of his sketches deal with the bore who tells a good story badly.

His life was in Montreal for only part of the year. For all his hatred of the farm of his youth, he had always longed for the country while he was away in the city. In 1908 he bought thirty-three acres on Lake Couchiching near Orillia. Old Brewery Bay (the name was Leacock's choice) is a lovely inlet with beautiful views across the lake. The first summer, he built a small shack—Leacock was a good carpenter—but in time he intended to have a very large, English-style country house and indeed did.

Leacock developed a routine which he largely kept for the rest of his life. He left McGill for Old Brewery Bay in the spring, a few days too early, said one colleague, from the point of view of his superiors, and came back, this time a few days too late, in the early fall. His summers followed the same sacrosanct pattern of writing, entertaining, gardening, building, and messing about in boats. He loved sailing, although he frequently got becalmed and had to run up his shirt for someone to come and fetch him. His handyman eventually painted the bow of his boat red so it was easier to spot. And there was always fishing. Leacock loved fishing as much for the rituals with which he surrounded it as for the fish themselves. There was always a picnic in special boxes and always lots to drink. His favourite companion was Jake Gaudaur, once the world champion rower, but he liked anyone who was good-natured and wanted to talk fishing. As he said of the fishermen in Izaak Walton's the *Compleat Angler:* "They meet and go fishing together and they talk— or they can't go fishing, so they talk; or they come in from fishing and they talk. Some of us do it still."

Both the household in the country and the one in Montreal revolved around Leacock and his needs. He became increasingly set in his ways. He loved making lists and large charts, which he would put up on the walls. He would not use the telephone if he could possibly avoid it. He refused to learn to drive but insisted that his chauffeurs do no more than thirty-five miles an hour and that they stop whenever they came to a railway crossing to let him out to walk across. In Montreal he slept on an outside porch, even in the deep of winter; inevitably of course he got locked out one night and nearly froze trying to get in to breakfast. He was affable—children loved him because he did not talk down to them, and the great English writer J.B. Priestley found him "immediately and immensely likeable"—but he preferred to see people on his own terms. He loved entertaining at his own houses and often spent a lot of time organizing the decorations and writing out the menu for his guests so that they would not, he hoped, get too many surprises. When it was time for him to go to bed, though, he would simply leave his guests to enjoy themselves. He liked formality—even in the country he expected everyone to dress for dinner—but, as with his own way of dressing, there was always something slightly absurd and untidy about it. Hors d'œuvres at his dinners might be sardines out of a tin or a whole cucumber.

Leacock, said those who knew him, always gave the impression of bursting with ideas and plans. When he wanted something done, he wanted it done immediately. He could be short-tempered; his wife tried to be out of the way when the monthly bills for groceries arrived at Old Brewery Bay. One evening when things did not go the way he wanted, he fired all the maids. The next day he hired them back and increased their pay.

He was at heart a kind and generous person. Although he sometimes appeared to be obsessed with making money, he also gave considerable amounts away. (And he made less than he might have done because he frequently wrote articles and gave lectures for free.) He supported the less fortunate members of his family, including his mother. During the Depression, he made work projects for people around Orillia and hired his servants' relatives. When he met by chance a young boy who had dropped out of school to run his father's second-hand bookshop in Montreal, Leacock became a patron, giving him advice on reading and buying quantities of books. Louis Melzack went on to found the Classic Books chain, which eventually had more than one hundred stores in Canada.

Increasingly Leacock became known as a character. This in part came naturally. His brothers George and Charlie were known for their eccentricities around Orillia. "They were very clever people, the Leacocks," said a woman who worked for Stephen. "But I think they were just overbrained and that's the only way I can put it. That's why they were a little queer." Everyone who knew him had stories of Stephen Leacock's absent-mindedness: the time he forgot to plug the drain in his new boat and it sank; the day students found him shovelling snow into his house; the dinner party where he had put on a black tie all right but had forgotten to change out of an old checked suit. There was also something theatrical, though, a sense that Leacock the curmudgeon or Leacock the absent-minded professor or, when he was at Old Brewery Bay, the country gentleman or the simple farmer were roles he had adopted. How often did he really throw his letters out his office window in the faith that some passerby would post them? But it made a good story. The different roles, the affability, and the sociability overlay the shyness and reserve that his niece Barbara Nimmo and others close to him noticed.

For all his success, he could be surprisingly sensitive. He was deeply hurt when the student paper at McGill had a satirical piece about Leaky Steamcock. He once argued that having a sense of humour was a mixed blessing: "A humorous person, I think, would be apt to be cut more nearly to the heart by unkindness, more deeply depressed by adversity, more elated by sudden good fortune, than a person with but little of that quick sense of contrast and incongruity which is the focus of the humorous point of view." Shortly before he died, he warned young writers that authors have to be prepared to be hurt. "The refusal of a first manuscript comes as such a crushing blow to self-confidence and self-belief that there is a danger that it may annihilate all further attempts."

Barbara Nimmo also thought that her uncle had trouble entering into festive occasions such as Christmas. In his stories, Christmas is often a disappointment. "This Santa Claus business is played out," starts "Hoodoo McFiggin's Christmas," one of Leacock's better-known stories. "It's a sneaking, underhand method and the sooner it's exposed the better." The unfortunate young hero longs for lovely toys and a puppy and gets instead a dreary collection of useful things.

Leacock used to tell the story of the man who went to see his doctor to complain of being sad. The cure was quite simple, the doctor thought; his patient should go and see the great clown, Grimaldi. "But I am Grimaldi," came the reply. Like many very funny people, Leacock had a strong strain of pessimism and melancholy. "You'd catch him at an off-moment," Carl Goldenberg remembered, "and there'd be this set look of sadness on his face." Leacock's view of life, at least at times, was gloomy. "Each of us in life is a prisoner," he wrote in 1935, oddly enough in his book on humour. "We are set and bound in our confined lot. Outside, somewhere, is eternity; outside, somewhere, is infinity." In the end, the universe was bound to end, taking all life with it. "All ends with a cancellation of forces and comes to nothing; and our universe ends thus with one vast, silent, unappreciated joke." Although Leacock believed in churches as useful institutions, he found no comfort in religion. In his view, he told his young son, Stevie, there is no existence after death. "Those who can believe these things are happy in the comfort of them, and die happy in them.... But those of us who cannot believe them must find our salvation elsewhere." What may have kept him going was a deeply engrained sense that it was simply wrong to despair.

Perhaps his well-known fondness for drink helped Leacock to cope both with his own shyness and with his bleak view of the world. Or perhaps he just liked the taste and the effects. He drank a glass of water once, he wrote, and it was pretty good, "almost like gin." His students claimed they could tell how much he had had to drink by the condition of his tie; slightly crooked meant only a few, but if it was tossed back over his shoulder, he had taken a lot. No one ever saw him drunk, although his face got red and he became chattier and a bit louder. When he travelled, he always made sure that he had a flask with him. When a customs officer once tried to prevent him from carrying his alcohol into the United States, where he was to speak, he simply cabled the organizers of his lecture in Buffalo: "No hooch, no spooch." Somehow, because it was the famous Stephen Leacock, things were arranged satisfactorily.

# CHAPTER FIVE

# Humour Is a Serious Business

Today we have theories of humour and indices of happiness, university workshops on humour and laughter, and international symposiums on the joke. It is a serious business trying to figure out what makes something funny. Leacock himself tried his hand at it repeatedly in articles and in books. Like a lot of very funny people, he wanted to be taken seriously. As an academic and public intellectual, he may have even been slightly embarrassed by the fact that he was better known for his humorous pieces than for his serious books and articles. What he has to say about humour has flashes of insight, but, alas, it is on the whole repetitive, dull, and incoherent.

When he writes seriously about humour, Leacock sounds like himself in another mood, caricaturing the pretentious academic. He dissects humour like a worm in a laboratory and festoons his analysis with quotations from Aristotle to Kant. He explains the physiology of the laugh. In his 1935 book, *Humour: Its Theory and Technique,* he solemnly lists and explains such techniques of the humorist as the pun, bad spelling, meiosis, and hyperbole. Parodies, he tells his readers, come in several forms, each better than the first. The straight verbal copies something already written; the imitation reproduces the original to show its faults; and, the highest of all, the parody holds a whole age up to ridicule. To show what he means, he includes examples, written specifically for the purpose, of his own humour. Unfortunately they fall far short of his best work. In *Humour and Humanity,* a book he wrote in 1937 which used some of the material from the earlier one, he tries to pin down the techniques still more, listing the different types of humorous situations or the varieties of humorous verse. The assiduous student, he suggests in both books, can learn how to be funny through careful study and practice. In his introduction to *Humour: Its Theory and Technique,* he wrote, "If this book turns out, as it probably will, to be one of those epoch making volumes which create a revolution in human thought, it will be followed by the establishment of regular college departments in humour." Is he joking?

Leacock bases much of his theory of humour on dubious science and equally dubious history. Although the Victorian faith in the progress and the steady evolution of human beings and human society from the primitive to the highly developed had already been severely undermined by the time Leacock was going to university, he continued to maintain, even in his two books on humour published in the 1930s, that humour had evolved in the same way. Primitive man laughed at his friends slipping on banana peels or his enemies getting their skulls smashed in, but the people of the twentieth century disdain "merriment of the lower type" in favour of gentle laughter at the complexities of life. "It becomes a condition of amusement that no serious harm or injury shall be inflicted but that only the appearance or simulation of it shall appear." In his 1916 essay on American humour, Leacock tried to make the argument that primitive humour was anti-social and necessarily disappeared over time by a sort of natural selection: "It runs counter to other instincts, those of affection, pity, unselfishness, upon which the progressive development of the race has largely depended." (Leacock excuses his idol Mark Twain for his savage humour about the American West on the grounds that the frontier in some ways reproduced primitive life.) In his gallop through the history, Leacock briskly dismisses the humour of the Greeks and Romans as "poor stuff." Who could think Aristophanes witty when it takes half a page of notes to explain one of his jokes? The Middle Ages were equally unfunny with their pedantic plays on words, and Chaucer is seriously overrated. Leacock grants that Shakespeare and Molière were humorists of the highest class, "But it is still the eminence of the single mountain, all the taller for its isolation."

While he argues at times that all humour is essentially the same, at others he sees something special in American humour—and he includes Canadian under that heading. The humour of the New World, he says, relies on its fresh approach; unlike European humour, it is not bound by tradition and convention. In Mark Twain's *Innocents Abroad,* the American travellers see the absurdities of European society. Leacock has a warning, though, for his fellow humorists: "Freedom of convention runs into crudity and coarseness, and a tone of cheap vulgarity is introduced calculated to discredit grievously the literature to which it belongs." He deplores Mark Twain's "Cannibalism in the Cars"; it is actually a very funny and rather savage story of how a group of congressmen marooned in a snowstorm use congressional procedures to see who will be eaten first.

Leacock always maintained that the best sort of humour was dignified and gentle. The true essence of humour, the first sentence of *Humour and Humanity* maintains, is "the kindly contemplation of the incongruities of life and the artistic expression thereof." It must be, he said in his 1916 essay, "Humour As I See It," without harm and without malice. Humour helps human beings to understand themselves. Although he insists on seeing humour as good-natured and kindly, Leacock cannot entirely avoid a tone of melancholy and even pessimism. Humour, he insisted, can help us deal with disappointment, for example, when we look at the gulf between what we hope for in life and what we actually achieve. It can smooth over the pains and the storms of life. "The fiercest anger cools; the bitterness of hate sleeps in the churchyard; and over it all there spread Time's ivy and Time's roses, preserving nothing but what is fair to look upon." At times Leacock sounds less like the genial humorist and more like the Stoics, who, as he must have known from his classical education, believed in sub-duing the emotions with reason and contemplating the vicissitudes of life with indifference. "Humour," he writes in the 1916 essay, "is blended with pathos till the two are one, and represent, as they have in every age, the mingled her-itage of tears and laughter that is our lot on earth." He made the same point every time he returned to the subject. Is he protesting too much?

In his disquisitions on humour, Leacock dismisses or ignores the humorists who do not fit his definition of humour as kindly. He says virtually nothing about Swift or Voltaire. He consigns the connection between cruelty and humour to the dustbin of history or argues it away as a vulgar aberration. "I admit," he says, though, "that there is in all of us a certain vein of the old demoniacal humour or joy in the misfortune of another which sticks to us like original sin." And that vein, although he may not have seen it, is present in his own writing. His humour often plays on human insecurities. "My Financial Career" appeals to us in part because we all feel apprehensive when we have to deal with large and imposing institutions and because we secretly fear making fools of ourselves. We can laugh at the unfortunate narrator as he rushes from the bank with the roars of laughter going up behind him, partly because it is not us. In "The Awful Fate of Melpomenus Jones," the hero finds himself trapped by his own inability to say goodbye when he goes to pay a brief social call. "Can't you stay a little longer?" or "Must you leave?" his hosts ask politely, and he stays for days, getting more and more distraught. Eventually he is carried upstairs in a delirium and after a month dies. "They say that when the last moment came, he sat up in bed with a beautiful smile of confidence playing upon his face, and said, 'Well—the angels are calling me; I'm afraid I really must go now.'"

Leacock moreover did not listen to his own advice when he said of humour "nor should it convey even incidentally any real picture of sorrow or suffering or death." In the cheerful little Mariposa of *Sunshine Sketches,* Leacock allows sadness to creep in. Jefferson Thorpe, the town's barber, makes a fortune in a mining boom and becomes a hero to the townspeople. He makes plans to send his beautiful daughter to drama school and to give away a huge chunk to the poor. He loses all his money in a crooked speculation and creeps quietly back to his barbershop. "Have you ever seen," asks the narrator, "an animal that is stricken through, how quiet it seems to move?" He is luckier than young Fizzlechip, who shoots himself. Or there is the irascible Judge Pepperleigh, who, we learn, mourns over his useless son who was killed in the Boer War. No one will ever tell the judge that the boy he idolized signed up for the army while he was drunk.

Leacock's touch is usually light, but there is often a real sting in his depiction of society. Hoodoo McFiggin's Christmas is ruined through the carelessness and selfishness of his parents. "How We Kept Mother's Day" is a comic story which contrasts the self-satisfaction of the children and the husband in arranging a special outing and a special dinner for the mother with the reality that she does all the work. The family decides that the trip in a hired car would be too tiring for her; instead she is told to have "a lovely restful day around the house." She also can look after the lavish dinner which is waiting for them as they arrive late from their glorious day of fishing. "Mother had to get up and down a good bit during the meal fetching things back and forward," says the narrator, "but at the end Father noticed it and he said she simply mustn't do it, that he wanted her to spare herself, and he got up and fetched the walnuts over from the sideboard himself." As the family goes off to bed (Mother of course has done the dishes), she tells them all she has had a wonderful day, "and I think there were tears in her eyes."

Selfishness is one of Leacock's targets. So are the well-intentioned who cause havoc to others. Mr. Butt, in the 1915 story "The Hallucination of Mr. Butt," is convinced that he is helping others. He drives a young couple, the Everleigh-Joneses, to distraction by insisting on visiting them late at night to help them settle in to their new house. After he has taken down all their pictures and rearranged the furniture, he decides that they should live much closer to the centre of the town. Powerless before his enthusiasm, they move. The husband falls into a delirium and nearly dies. The narrator sees a man with a hunted face asking the hall porter at his club whether Mr. Butt is in the club and who dashes for the door when the answer is yes. "That's a new member, sir," says the porter, "Mr. Everleigh-Jones."

Hypocrisy was another Leacock target. He firmly advised his young son before his confirmation that he should not profess to believe things that he did not. "It is for you to decide. Unbelief is a burden, but the pretence of belief, hypocrisy, is death to all that is decent in you." In *Arcadian Adventures with the Idle Rich,* the tycoon Lucullus Fyshe talks contemptuously over lunch at his club about the wickedness of the British aristocracy. "How the working class, the proletariat, stand for such tyranny is more than I can see." He hopes, says Fyshe, that there will be a revolution in Britain that will put an end to the whole thing. At that point his waiter brings him asparagus that he finds too cold. Fyshe sends it back at once and says to his table companion that the club staff, "these pampered fellows," are getting unbearable. "By gad," he exclaims, "if I had my way I'd fire the whole lot of them; lock 'em out, put 'em on the street." Fyshe is the same man who exposes the corruption at city hall by offering its employees bribes. He is equally as self-righteous when they take the money as when they do not.

In Leacock's world, virtue is rarely rewarded. In *Arcadian Adventures,* Peter Spillikins, the foolish, good-hearted, and very rich young man, turns away from his true love to marry the dazzling Mrs. Everleigh, whose sons, by some strange chance, are only a few years younger than he himself. While Spillikins plays billiards with his stepsons, his wife amuses herself with her lover, Captain Cormorant. Spillikins thinks he is perfectly happy while the kind and good young woman whom he should have married sits broken-hearted in a darkened room. It is hard to find the kindness and absence of malice in the story.

Robertson Davies, who knew a thing or two about writing funny pieces, thought it was a mistake to try to analyze Leacock's humour too much. (He also thought that, at his best, Leacock was a genius.) Leacock himself in *Humour: Its Theory and Technique* also warned: "To analyze is often to destroy." The best way to appreciate his work is simply to read it—but to read with care. Leacock wrote a lot of humorous pieces that were not all that funny. He thought, for example, that *Nonsense Novels,* his series of spoofs he published in 1911, was among the funniest things he ever wrote. Today they seem painfully laboured and arch. Part of the trouble is that in this and many of his other parodies the works that he was taking off are long since forgotten.

When Leacock is angry, about prohibition, for example, his humour can be too broad and too crude. The title piece of his 1919 book, *The Hohenzollerns in America,* starts from the amusing conceit that the German royal family takes refuge in the United States as penniless refugees after Germany's defeat in the First World War but goes downhill because Leacock cannot keep his light touch. "The proper punishment," says Leacock in his preface, "for the Hohenzollerns, and the Hapsburgs, and the Mecklenburgs, and the Muckendorfs, and all such puppets and princelings, is that they should be made to work." The resulting sketch is nasty and not at all funny. At its end, the former Kaiser, now a ragged street peddler in the Bowery, dies of his injuries after a traffic accident.

At the other end of the scale are the great classics, "Boarding-House Geometry," for example, or "My Financial Career." Everyone who likes Leacock has his or her favourite. One of mine is "A, B, and C: The Human Element in Mathematics," which starts with the brilliant and mad assumption that the letters in mathematical problems are really human beings. *A* is energetic and strong-willed. He likes to dig ditches twice as fast as everyone else or walk three times farther. *B* is rather nice and gentle and knows that he can never compete with *A*. *C* is frail and exhausted and always behind in everything. Even in the collections which most critics agree are not his best, such as *Short Circuits,* published in 1928, there are always gems.

"The Man with the Adventure Story," for example, is a lovely sketch of a man on a train with a genuinely interesting story who keeps being interrupted by the assembled bores. His mention that he is lost in a pine forest in the middle of winter brings an animated discussion about the price of wood, and when he introduces a wolf, that in turn leads to an argument over the price of fur. The unfortunate raconteur never finishes his story.

In 1912 Leacock published what many think is his masterpiece—*Sunshine Sketches of a Little Town.* It came about as the result of fortuitous timing. Leacock was looking for something to follow up *Nonsense Novels,* and the *Montreal Star* wanted to do a series on a small Canadian town. B.K. Sandwell, a former student and friend of Leacock who had become a successful journalist in Montreal, arranged a meeting between Leacock and the editor. The paper commissioned twelve articles and gave what was, for Canada, a very generous payment. If the offer had come a few months later, in Sandwell's view, when Leacock had become better known in the United States and was being offered a range of lucrative deals, he might well have turned down the local paper. The articles, a series of stories about life in a small Ontario town called Mariposa, which is very like the Orillia that Leacock knew so well, appeared in the first part of 1912 and then, as was now Leacock's practice, as a book shortly afterwards in Canada, Great Britain, and the United States. He was pleased, Leacock told his British publisher John Lane, that the price was reasonable. "I think humorous stuff ought to be cheap; those who are most willing to buy it are young people with lots of life and fun in them and, as a rule, not too much money. Rich people buy stuff with a gorgeous cover & fine paper, and never read it."

*Sunshine Sketches* was an instant success and has remained in print ever since. The reviews were, as for Leacock's first two books, overwhelmingly enthusiastic. "Pure mirth," said the *Chicago Record-Herald.* "We cannot recall a more laughable book," said the *Pall Mall Gazette,* while *The Spectator* thought it showed "a most welcome freedom from the pessimism of Old-World fiction." Part of the book's charm for readers outside Canada was that it was so very Canadian. Leacock had been very conscious of that as he was writing it. "I can make it Canadian enough to English readers," he assured John Lane, "by inserting a sentence or two here and there." In Canada, the book appealed because it was about the small towns which were intensely familiar to so many Canadians and yet were starting to change.

When the Leacock family first came to Canada in the 1870s, farms were isolated but so too were the small towns.

Roads were not going to be paved until the time of the First World War. Leacock remembered the slow struggle along the dirt tracks which turned into swamps in the spring or the corduroy ones where logs laid side by side provided footing of a sort for the horses. In Central Canada, waterways, both natural and man-made, linked towns such as Mariposa with the outside world but, thanks to the winters, only for part of the year. The railway network which was starting to transform Canada was in its infancy. (Mariposa takes great pride that it is on the main line, even though the trains whistle through without stopping.) Telegraphs were expensive and cumbersome, and telephones were not going to appear outside the big cities until the 1880s.

The last decades of the nineteenth century brought increasingly rapid change, especially in the more settled parts of Canada such as southern Ontario. The first automobile causes a sensation when it roars into Mariposa. And the town now has its own railway line to the big city a hundred miles to the south. It also has its own telephone exchange with its four women operators sitting on high stools, "jabbing the connecting plugs in and out as if electricity cost nothing." It is a matter of local pride that Mariposa has electricity. The power comes, like Orillia's did, from a local hydro plant, but by the time it reaches the little light bulbs, the light looks as blurry as the light of the old coal oil lamps.

Mariposa knows about the outside world even if the outside world does not know much about Mariposa. In small towns, says the narrator, people have lots of time to read the newspapers cover to cover. In Jefferson Thorpe's barbershop they talk about the future of China or the relations between the German Kaiser and his parliament. Some Mariposans go away to college; the local Member of Parliament had two sessions at one years ago and that makes him a man of learning. And the outside world, from time to time, impinges on Mariposa. In the spring, the rough lumbermen, some of whom are local farm boys, come down from the north and lie about drunk on the sidewalk outside the hotel. The discovery of minerals to the north creates great excitement. (Sudbury's nickel and copper were found in the 1880s; silver at Cobalt in the 1900s; and gold was struck at Kirkland Lake in 1911 as Leacock was writing his sketches.) The mining boom lures Mariposa's savings and its more adventurous men. Some of its sons go to fight in the South African war; many more, although no one knows it, will fight and die in the First World War.

Mariposa exists in a specific time and a specific place. It could not be anywhere else but southern Ontario. Its people are of British stock, many of them descended from the Loyalists who left the United States after the American Revolution. They are Protestant as far as we know. We scarcely hear about Catholics or Irish immigrants. The two main churches are the Anglican and the Presbyterian. The Salvation Army is the only representative of a more enthusiastic sort of religion. Political affiliations are more important and interesting than religious ones. Most people in Mariposa, and this is true still in some parts of southern Ontario, are lifelong Liberals or Conservatives. The Canadian novelist Guy Vanderhaeghe, who grew up in the West, said Leacock helped him to understand why his Ontario grandfather always voted for the Conservative party in Saskatchewan even though it had no hope of winning. "He followed this fine old Ontario tradition of being born with one's politics decided." Some Mariposans, though, will switch their votes if there is something in it for them. The only thing you cannot do, says the narrator, is have no politics at all. Such people, the general opinion is, are up to something funny.

Leacock's Mariposa takes itself seriously. (So does Orillia still; its website says endearingly, "From our shores we can go anywhere in the world.") In the Reciprocity Election of 1911, over whether Canada would have more or less trade with the United States, Mariposa, Loyalist Mariposa, votes overwhelmingly against. That, in the view of the locals, saves the British Empire. And no one should think, the narrator warns, that Mariposa is a dull place. The round of amusements, from the Fireman's Ball to the town band in the park, is simply dazzling. On warm summer evenings the drugstore blazes out as a major social centre. "There is such a laughing and a talking as you never heard, and the girls are all in white and pink and cambridge blue, and the soda fountain is of white marble with silver taps, and it hisses and sputters, and Jim Eliot and his assistant wear white coats with red geraniums in them, and it's just as gay as gay. The foyer of the opera in Paris may be a fine sight, but I doubt if it can compare with the inside of Eliot's drug store in Mariposa—for real gaiety and joy of living."

As in all small towns, people tend to know all about one another. Everyone knows that Peter Pupkin, the bank teller, is courting Zena Pepperleigh, the judge's daughter. After all, he takes her out in his canoe in the evening and "for fun" they go once to the Presbyterian church, "which if you know Mariposa, you realize to be a wild sort of escapade that ought to speak volumes." A high-school teacher is widely known as "the one who drank" because he has an occasional beer. One of the few figures of mystery is the hotelkeeper, Josh Smith, who, it was said, had started out as a cook in the lumber camps up north. Smith is huge and imposing, his face "solemn, inexpressible, unreadable, the face of the heaven-born hotel keeper." Only the faithful Billy, his clerk, knows that he is illiterate. Smith is the Napoleon and the Bismarck of Mariposa, pulling his own chestnuts and those of the town out of the fire (sometimes, as in the case of the Anglican church, literally). Through masterly and devious means, Smith saves his own liquor licence and wins the election as the Conservative candidate. He salvages the *Mariposa Belle* when it sinks. He leads the effort to keep the town from burning when the Anglican church goes up in flames. (The fact that he was seen carrying a can of kerosene toward the church the night of the fire is an odd story which no one believes—or admits to believing.)

Leacock drops other hints that there is a darker side to life and more below the surface in Mariposa than first appears, as when he talks of Judge Pepperleigh's son, who died fighting in South Africa, or how the barber, Jefferson Thorpe, loses his fortune. The widowed Reverend Drone, of the Anglican church, is a great comic figure as he bumbles about to the Mother's Union or the Infant Class. He takes great pride in his Gold Medal for Greek, won fifty years ago, and is often seen sitting in his garden with a Greek volume in hand. He cannot translate anything, he says, because the true beauty would be lost. But kindly, good Dean Drone is haunted by the growing debt on his magnificent new church. When it looks like nothing can be done to save the parish from bankruptcy, he struggles to compose his letter of resignation. While he is at his desk, he sees the glow of flames leaping from the church and falls forward with a stroke. All is saved in a sense; as it turns out the church carries a lot of insurance. Drone is never the same, however. He sits in his garden reading Greek easily because, he says, his head is so much clearer. "And sometimes,—when his head is very clear,—as he sits there reading beneath the plum blossoms he can hear them singing beyond, and his wife's voice."

In Mariposa, though, things usually turn out well. The sun generally shines on the little town. There is no poverty and no crime. Disagreements over politics never result in permanent rifts. The dentist and the doctor own a motor boat together; during the big election they agree to take it out on separate Saturdays. Peter Pupkin becomes a hero and wins Zena Pepperleigh. They live happily ever after in their "enchanted" house with their "enchanted" baby.

Just as Garrison Keillor does with Lake Wobegon, Leacock is mocking Mariposa's foibles, its follies, and its frequent hypocrisies. He does so with affection and perhaps a certain regret that he cannot go back to the more innocent times of his youth. *Sunshine Sketches* ends with a short afterword, this time seen from the perspective of the city. Did you not know, the narrator asks his reader, that there is a little train that leaves the main station every day for Mariposa? You knew about it when you were the boy who had just arrived in the city, but as the years have passed and you have prospered, you have forgotten all about it. In that, you are like the other successful men who you meet in the grand Mausoleum Club. "Would you believe it that practically every one of them came from Mariposa once upon a time, and that there isn't one of them that doesn't sometimes dream in the dull quiet of the long evening here in the club, that some day he will go back and see the place." If you do go back, the narrator warns, you will find it the same, but you will have changed.

Leacock always maintained that his town of Mariposa was completely fictional, but he took much from Orillia, which he had come to know well as he was growing up and which was the closest town to his summer home. Before the First World War, Orillia had some 5,000 inhabitants; Mariposa had the same (although its people always suspected they were undercounted in a malicious plot to do them down). Orillia had two newspapers—the *News-Letter* and the *Packet and Times;* Mariposa had one—the *Newspacket.* In Orillia, the town barber was Jeff Short; in Mariposa, he was Jeff Thorpe. In *Sunshine Sketches,* Golgotha Gingham is the successful undertaker. "I have often heard him explain," says the narrator, "that to associate with the living, uninteresting though they appear, is the only way to secure the custom of the dead." Horace Bingham, the real Orillia undertaker, said mildly that he thought this made him sound a bit too preoccupied with business. Not all the reaction in Orillia was so mild. A lot of its prominent citizens never forgave Leacock, and his own mother scolded him for his caricature of Canon Greene, the real Anglican clergyman, who was much loved in town. Greene himself lived up to his reputation for kindliness and apparently never bore Leacock a grudge for what was a pretty harsh portrait. Locals described Leacock as crazy or the town drunk, and it must be admitted that he gave them material to work on.

Robertson Davies believed that Leacock was so stung by the local reaction that his development as an artist, at least in one direction, was balked. In Davies's view, *Sunshine Sketches* has "the strong appearance of being the work of a man who will write a novel very soon." And certainly there are in the book, just as there are in the later *Arcadian Adventures with the Idle Rich,* some of the elements of a novel: good stories, vivid characters, and strong settings. When *Sunshine Sketches* first came out, Pelham Edgar, an old friend from Upper Canada days and later a distinguished professor of English, was convinced that Leacock possessed the combination of humour and acute observation that would lead him to write a series of outstanding novels. Leacock, when Edgar told him this, was surprised: personally he did not think *Sunshine Sketches* all that good. *Nonsense Novels,* his rather tiresome literary parodies, was, in Leacock's opinion, much better. "I remember," said Edgar, "saying in my protest that he was wasting his time in such sawdusty work, and that he was capable of producing a world masterpiece if he could only place some curb on his irrepressible humour." Leacock himself downplayed his potential as a novelist. "I can invent characters quite easily," he said after *Sunshine Sketches,* "but I have no notion as to how to make things happen to them. Indeed I see no reason why anything should."

Perhaps, though, Leacock, with his impatience and rush to get things wrapped up, was better fitted for the shorter humorous pieces than for more complicated and sustained plots. Perhaps too, his temperament made him disinclined to probe too deeply into human nature and the vicissitudes of human life. And perhaps, and it is a pity to think so, he was too tempted by the lucrative and quick returns made by his sketches to want to undertake the sustained and difficult work of writing a novel.

In his 1930 book, *Economic Prosperity in the British Empire,* Leacock protested against those who saw a Canadian school of writing "as a thing to be encouraged like Canadian cheese and Canadian apples." It was, he said, a misguided idea of patriotism. Nor, he wrote in 1941, is there a Canadian way of being funny. It is hard today not to see him as a very Canadian writer indeed. Certainly his Mariposa could not exist anywhere else outside southern Ontario at the turn of the last century. And in his ability to puncture pomposity, to show up hypocrisy, to mock the powerful and self-important, and to encourage Canadians to laugh at themselves, Leacock is surely one of the spiritual ancestors of Rick Mercer or the Royal Canadian Air Farce or, as they both recognized, of Robertson Davies and Mordecai Richler.

# CHAPTER SIX

# The Eccentric Professor

Leacock loved living in Montreal and he loved McGill. "I know of no more attractive scene," he wrote after his retirement, "than the campus of a college on the autumn day when the students gather for the new session—the commencement of another academic year. The sky is never so blue nor the still, fleecy clouds so white, nor the autumn leaves so bright with red and russet and yellow, as on that day." In his time at McGill, the university was small; it had only some 2,400 undergraduates in the 1920s and 1930s, something Leacock approved of. Toronto, he said, as a big provincial university, had to take all sorts. McGill did not: "McGill doesn't have to teach anybody. In medicine, McGill from the richness of its soil, restricts its crops as they restrict coffee in Brazil and hogs in Missouri."

For Leacock, university teaching was another world from the high schools where he had once worked. He had hated school teaching, in part because it was still too close to the genteel poverty of his childhood. In his unfinished autobiography, he goes on at length about the lot of the ambitious young man who tries to put himself through university by teaching. The details of salary, of the outlays for board and lodging, the price for getting a shirt washed, the expenses of college are all still vivid in Leacock's mind half a century later. So too is the terrible fear that the young teacher will not make it, that he will start to drink and gradually slide out of the middle classes in which he has such a precarious toehold. Even if he manages to hold his teaching job, he will not have the comfort of being as good as the next man. "I never was," wrote Leacock, "and never felt I was, in the ten years I was as a teacher." He was wrong, he admits in his autobiography, to have spent so much of his life condemning the profession. It is all right, he says half-heartedly, for those who are fitted for it. "The thing wrong is the setting we fail to give it."

The setting at McGill was right for Leacock. He regarded himself, as he wrote in the preface to *Sunshine Sketches,* as singularly fortunate and he was not joking when he added, "The emolument is so high as to place me distinctly above the policemen, postmen, street-car conductors, and other salaried officials of the neighbourhood, while I am able to mix with the poorer of the businessmen of the city on terms of something like equality." Although he made much more from his writing than he did from his McGill salary, he never contemplated giving up his university post. He liked the leisurely, predictable routine of a professor's life, and he found McGill highly congenial. Faculty dined and lunched with one another and gathered at the University Club for drinks after their day's work ended. No one thought it particularly odd that René du Roure, Leacock's great friend, would drop by his class a few minutes before Leacock's lecture was finished to take him off to the club for a game of billiards.

Another of Leacock's particular friends was Andrew Macphail, the professor of the history of medicine and himself a distinguished writer, who encouraged Leacock from the start of his writing career. The two men belonged to the Pen and Pencil Club, which brought together artists and writers to share their work. (John McCrae, author of one of Canada's most famous poems, "In Flanders Fields," was another member until he went off to the war in which he would die.) Leacock first tried out a number of his most famous pieces, such as "My Financial Career," in the club. Macphail also published his early work in the *University Magazine,* in its time the leading Canadian literary journal.

McGill allowed Leacock ample time for his growing writing and lecturing career. For much of his time at McGill, the principal was his great friend General Sir Arthur Currie, Canada's outstanding commander in the First World War. Currie, who had been Leacock's pupil years before when he was just starting out as a high-school teacher, admired the older man tremendously and thought him a real asset to McGill. Until Currie's death, Leacock was spared interference by the sort of university administrators he satirized, such as Dr. Boomer in *Arcadian Adventures with the Idle Rich*, who longed to fire all his professors. Although Leacock served as chair of the Department of Economics and Political Science for decades, his administrative duties were not heavy; in fact he largely ignored them and let a devoted younger colleague do most of the tedious work.

Leacock loved teaching and he was very fond of his students. He slipped them money when they ran short of funds. Although he used his own book on political economy in his classes because, he said, it was the only decent text, he insisted on refunding seventeen cents to each student who bought it from him so that he would not make any royalty money from them. He encouraged his students and lavished advice on them. "As to whether you will take English or Economics," he wrote to his student Eugene Forsey, "it is a very important decision to take & you must reflect well upon it. It affects not only your college course, but your 'hereafter.'" (Forsey's "hereafter" was as a distinguished academic and one of Canada's leading constitutional experts.) Leacock found his students jobs and wrote them glowing reference letters—in his own style. One of his students remembered how Leacock looked at the standard Harvard Business School reference form, with its lists of characteristics and boxes to check, with disbelief. "They can't expect a person like me to fill in a thing like this," Leacock said firmly as he drew a line across it. At the bottom of the page he simply wrote, "Mr. Pugsley has taken a good course with us at McGill and is qualified not only to enter your college but to adorn it." Because it was the famous Stephen Leacock, the reference worked beautifully.

Although the majority of students in his days were still men, increasingly he found himself teaching young women. In his writings on universities, he says repeatedly that he is not for coeducation. In his generally charming piece on Oxford, written in the early 1920s, he goes off on an extended rant about how women are changing, for the worse, the character of the place. He is only half joking when he says that Oxford has fallen away from the high academic ideals of the Middle Ages by admitting women. They are too attractive, too much of a distraction for the men. "The fundamental trouble," he concludes, "is that men and women are different creatures, with different minds and different aptitudes, and different paths in life." As so often with Leacock, though, he said one thing and did another. He treated women in his classes much as he did the men and, if they were bright, directed his questions at them. He helped them on in their careers. "Remember," he wrote in 1940 to a young woman, "if one thing fails, the next one doesn't and that for people who have brains and energy and youth, the world is still wide open." Anne Romoff Gross, who was among the pioneering women in law at McGill, found him by far the most encouraging and helpful of her undergraduate professors.

Leacock approached his teaching rather as he did his writing. He dashed at it and did not bother much with the details. He thought university regulations tedious. North American professors, he said, were expected to be like shepherds with their students. "They all go humping together over the hurdles with the professor chasing them with a set of 'tests' and 'recitations', 'marks' and 'attendances', the whole operation obviously copied from the time-clock of the business man's factory." He particularly disliked having to take attendance in his classes. Under McGill's regulations, if students did not show up, they failed. When one particularly dilatory student had a last chance to attend a lecture,

Leacock apparently forgot about the roll call and started to lecture. Students heard slow footsteps approaching and then a chair squeaking as someone sat down. Now, Leacock announced, the time had come to take attendance. The whole class burst into applause.

His lectures—given in his tattered, ancient gown—were famous on the McGill campus as performances. Students who were not enrolled in his courses would attend for the show. "When we entered the classroom for political science," an American student recalled, "we were all agog with curiosity. Up to the professor's desk shuffled an untidy, dishevelled figure, apparently just risen from a night on a park bench...." Leacock was also famous for going off on a tangent in his lectures. One of his students remembered the day the word *chaos* came up in the class. Leacock traced the etymology back to Dutch and then wandered on to the Dutch settlers in southern Africa. "The whole lecture," said the student, "was taken up with the history of South Africa, without any reference whatsoever to the purpose of that particular lecture." What students took away from Leacock's course was another matter. When he looked at his lecture notes before the final examination, one student remembered, they were completely useless. Perhaps Leacock was defending himself when he wrote, "One queer teacher—

something of a crank and eccentric—may be of more cultural value than a whole boxful as alike as ninepins."

For many, Leacock was the most marvellous professor they had ever encountered. He was a genius *manqué*, Eugene Forsey thought: "He did actually inspire, stimulate, arouse, awake, stab people's minds broad awake...." Leacock was impressive, too, in his fairness. One student, later a prominent lawyer, submitted a paper disagreeing with Leacock's views on empire. Leacock gave it an extraordinary 98 percent. The student tried to apologize for disagreeing with his professor: "Tut, tut," Leacock replied. "I don't expect my students to agree with me. I like them to give me their honest views, and I really enjoyed your paper." Conservative in his own political views, Leacock always made sure that his students knew the other side. During the Depression, he handed out a reading list so inclusive of left-wing viewpoints that some of his students became radicals.

Leacock's own views about academic life were ambivalent. He complains about universities being undervalued by society, but then turns around and laughs at them for being silly and unworldly, or simply ineffective. At times, when he extols the marvellous life of the mind and the peace of the campus, he sounds as though he would like to live in the ivory tower forever. At others, he resembles the businessmen he so frequently caricatures talking about the "real" world, which of course lies outside the university. "Paradise Lost," the speech he made as he retired from McGill, is typical of his ambivalence. Professors, he says, are often comic figures, "gullible to the point of imbecility," but, on the other hand, they represent "that higher idealism lifted above life." Graduates who look back at their old universities from the hurly-burly of their busy lives will glimpse another, better world. Being Leacock, he immediately undercut this revelation of his deep feelings about the value of academic life with a joke. He was glad, he said, that his friends had clubbed together to give a set of his works to the McGill library; his books cost at least a dollar while as for Shakespeare, you could get his works for only fifteen cents each.

In his views on what made the ideal university, Leacock is both vague and romantic. There are two ways to learn, he says (and it is easy to tell which he prefers). There is the organized, disciplined way, where subjects are approached methodically, and students submit work and write examinations, or the spontaneous, natural, free way, where the students, and scholars, follow their own instincts. "We are moved and stimulated to understanding far more by our imagination than by our intellect," he writes in his afterword to *Hellements of Hickonomics*. Oxford, he says, is wonderful because "It has no order, no arrangement, no systems." There are no modern courses such as you get at North American universities, no domestic science or business. At Oxford, students sit with their tutor as he talks and smokes his pipe: "Men who have been systematically smoked at for four years turn into ripe scholars."

Oxford, for Leacock, hearkens back to a largely imaginary past where blissfully happy scholars followed their studies, searching only for the truth and unworried by the passage of time or the tumult of the world outside. That was the ideal university—the one that wanted to mould its students' characters and make them better people who want only to search for truth. Give him the freedom to build a university from scratch and about fifty wooded acres, Leacock cries in "On the Need for a Quiet College," and he will start with a few buildings, some books, and, the most important thing, professors who love learning and teaching in equal parts. His professors will not have to sit on committees or bother with administration. Students will come for the sheer love of learning and they will study only the humanities, not subjects like commerce or medicine. In his ideal university, as he said elsewhere, students would find "a maximum of stimulation and a minimum of examination." (And there would be no women to distract them.)

The debates about the purpose and proper character of the university have existed as long as there have been universities, and Leacock's concerns are still very much alive today. We still worry today about the quality of our undergraduates, about whether it is better for them to do good liberal arts courses or get down at once to professional training that will presumably get them jobs. We worry too about whether society truly values universities and, conversely, about whether universities are engaged enough with society. Although he would not have known the term, like Leacock we worry about universities becoming "politically correct." "Students and studies are already being ironed out as flat as rolled steel in a Pittsburgh mill," he complained. "In the time to come, all the colleges will be utterly and absolutely like. The rich variations of senility and imbecility which marked the professoriate of old days will all be gone. Each professor will be as neat as a tailor's dummy. At the first sign of aberration he will be pensioned off to where he can do no harm."

Whether business had an excessive influence on universities, including his own McGill, was something else Leacock worried about. (The relations between powerful business interests and universities are also issues that have not gone away in the twenty-first century.) In *Arcadian Adventures* he satirizes the wealthy donors who like to attach strings to their donations. As Dr. Boomer, the president of the local university, shows around a potential donor, he proudly points to the busts of the tycoons who have already made their donations. There, dressed as a Roman senator, for example, is Mr. Underbugg, "who founded our lectures on the Four Gospels on the sole stipulation that henceforth any reference of ours to the four gospels should be coupled with his name." When a prominent Montreal businessman, William Massey Birks, suggested to Leacock in the 1930s that university professors should not express radical ideas such as support for socialism, Leacock sent him a firm letter in defence of academic freedom. If a professor made propaganda in his classes, in favour of socialism, nudism, or anything else he pleased, then clearly he was breaking his contract, but otherwise, Leacock told Birks, professors should have the same rights as anyone else to hold what opinions they wanted.

Leacock also disliked the growth of business studies, which he ascribed to the desire of universities to kowtow to the business classes. He wrote in a 1913 article for *University Magazine:*

> The result was that a great number of tin-pot institutions and two penny departments began to turn out a new kind of graduate, who spelt Caesar with

a G and thought that Edmund Burke was the name of a brewer. Over the surface of the graduate's mind was spread a thin layer of practical knowledge brittle as ginger bread.

Leacock deplored the proliferation of professional courses altogether. "Education," he complained in 1939, "has become to a great extent a mere acquirement of a legal qualification to enter a closed profession, in place of a process undertaken for its own sake."

Another Leacock target was what he described as "the bossy and brutal interference from above." Universities were getting too many regulations, too many forms, and too many bureaucrats. A university president used to be a distinguished scholar; now, said Leacock in his piece on Oxford, he is "a busy, hustling person, approximating as closely to a business man as he can do it." Dr. Boomer, who is one of Leacock's great comic inventions, has built lavish new buildings for the faculties of industrial and mechanical science, while hidden away behind them a dignified but dilapidated old building houses the faculty of arts. Boomer has transformed the university:

It offered such a vast variety of themes, topics, and subjects to the students, that there was nothing

> that a student was compelled to learn, while from
> its own presses in its own press-building it sent out
> a shower of bulletins and monographs like driven
> snow from a rotary plow.

Yet even as he laughs at the Boomers of the world, Leacock gets in some digs at the professors too, for example, at what he sees as their laziness. When he looked back on his years of teaching, Leacock maintained that he would have chosen no other profession in the world. In the right sort of university, "a professor's life in its outlook touches as close to eternity as any form of existence still with us." At other times and in other moods, though, he sounds like one of the philistine Arcadian rich. He knows a man, he says in his sketch of the ideal university, who spent twenty-four years working on the Italian political philosopher Machiavelli before he dared to publish a book—and who then felt guilty for rushing into print too soon. He lauds the dedicated, unworldly scholar who devotes his life to a subject, but he undercuts his own praise with contempt. They study such things as the geography of Nineveh or the place names of the Yucatan. Sometimes, seemingly by mistake, they do something human. "Somewhere in such a professor's life he has picked up, more or less unnoticed, a wife, as a beaver picks up a mate way off in the woods." And what does the learning of such admirable scholars amount to? "When they tackle an author," Leacock wrote in *Too Much College,* "they dissect him from the head down and hang up the skin. They follow the tide of human thought from Plato downward till they almost, never quite, reach yesterday."

As a scholar himself, Leacock was never in danger of putting the world behind him or of losing himself in a single topic or discipline. Certainly not in economics. It is fair to say that Leacock was a better political scientist, even a better historian, than he was an economist. One of his students, Sydney David Pierce, who later became a distinguished Canadian diplomat, was grateful to Leacock for getting him a job teaching economics at Dalhousie University until he arrived and found that Leacock had taught him virtually nothing about the subject. Leacock's fellow economists made jokes about his grasp of the subject. Humorists, it was said, thought him an economist, and economists thought him a humorist. Philip Vineberg, who studied at McGill and later became a prominent lawyer in Montreal, said of Leacock: "He was not terribly concerned with modern economics as it was evolving at the time." The only work of the leading economist John Maynard Keynes that Leacock appeared to have read thoroughly was his polemic against the Treaty of Versailles of 1919, not the groundbreaking works in economics. (When Keynes was asked by an English publisher for his opinion on Leacock's 1931 book, *Economic Prosperity in the British Empire,* on how to deal with the Depression, he dismissed it as "extraordinarily commonplace" and recommended against publication.)

As an economist, Leacock was more interested in political economy, where economic forces met social, political or ideological ones. Indeed he criticized his fellow economists for ignoring them. Although he was dismissive of Thorstein Veblen, his former teacher at the University of Chicago, Leacock in fact resembled him in his interest in the interplay between society and its institutions, whether government or the legal system, and the forces which drove production such as technology. Economics, for Leacock, simply did not explain enough. Nor did it deal with the important questions. Why, for example, should a hard-working labourer earn a pittance and an idle rentier live in luxury? To Leacock, the profound problem facing the twentieth century was one of the fair distribution of society's goods. "Is the allotment correct," he asked in *The Unsolved Riddle of Social Justice.* "Is it fair or unfair, and does it stand for the true measure of social justice?"

As he had done earlier with classics and, to a lesser extent, with the study of languages, Leacock increasingly turned against his own subject. His students noticed that while he rarely made jokes in his political science lectures, he frequently used humour in his economics ones. For Leacock, increasingly, economics was not a serious subject. In his view, it was becoming too esoteric and too removed from the real world. It was a "hopeless muddle," he wrote in 1939, with its dependence on statistics, mathematics, specialized jargon, and, perhaps worst of all, psychology. Economists were making a great mistake, Leacock thought, in trying to quantify such things as value, preference, likes and dislikes. In an article he wrote for the *Atlantic Monthly* in 1936, he takes on Keynes for using mathematical formula (unwisely as it turns out because it is clear that Leacock has misunderstood Keynes's point). Rather than dealing seriously with the trend toward mathematics in economics, Leacock amuses himself in the article by imagining what well-known poems would look like if they were put in mathematical terms. "Mathematical economics," he concludes, "is what is called in criminal circles 'a racket.'" In the *Hellements of Hickonomics,* Leacock attacks everyone and everything, from Adam Smith to banking, in clumsy verse. "Forty years of hard work on economics," Leacock says in his preface, "has pretty well removed all the ideas I ever had about it. I think the whole science is a wreck and has got to be built up again."

His antipathy to economics as a discipline was further fuelled by the impact of the Depression, when economists did not seem able to come up with solutions for the collapse of capitalism. His fellow academics were largely useless, he wrote in his 1939 piece "Has Economics Gone to Seed?": "At a time when the world is in danger of collapse from the dilemma of wealth and want, the college economists can shed no light." He liked to repeat the joke about where all the economists would reach if they were laid out in a line from the Mexican border. The answer: nowhere.

Leacock's approach to economic problems was essentially a moral and political one: the rich ought to realize their duty to the poor and everyone ought to work hard and be virtuous. Adam Smith had been right for once, in Leacock's opinion, when he said that people worked with enthusiasm only when it was for themselves. Government regulation and intervention, though, was needed to temper the selfishness of unregulated capitalism. On the other hand, Leacock could never accept socialism. "But this socialism, this communism, would only work in Heaven where they don't need it, or in Hell where they have it already."

Leacock's only serious academic work in political science came early on in his career with his 1906 textbook, *Elements of Political Science.* It is a useful survey, directed at undergraduates, rather than a major contribution to what was a rapidly growing field. The fact that a new professor would boldly set out to describe the whole field shows something of Leacock's self-confidence. He never again carried out such a sustained piece of research and that in turn says something about his priorities as a professor. He was more interested in educating students and in taking part in the great public debates of his times than in doing research or talking to his fellow academics.

The focus of *Elements of Political Science* is the state, the methods and principles of government, and the ways in which power works, either legally or not, to force people to do certain things. In Leacock's day, that was a widely accepted definition of what political science was about. Today the definition has widened to include the study of all sorts of groups—from churches to labour unions—and relationships which involve coercion but also persuasion. Students at the universities where the Leacock text was adopted must have found it dry (there is no hint of the funny Stephen Leacock) but very useful. It goes briskly and clearly through the development of the state and the relations of states to one another; it classifies different types of government from the federal to the colonial; it examines the different parts and the different levels of government; and it looks at the ways in which the state, increasingly, is regulating society. Along the way, Leacock deals with thinkers such as Kant and Hobbes and such complex ideas as "sovereignty" and "liberty" and with the perennially important debate between those who believe that society and politics should be based on individualism and those who advocate collective approaches such as socialism.

While some of the book seems dated—in its extended discussion of colonial government for example—much of it deals with issues we still grapple with today. How do we strike a balance between the power of the state and the rights of the individual? Who has the final word? How should states deal with the poor and weak among their citizens? Is the international system an anarchic one in which states look out only for their own interests and where the only sure protection against aggression is to be strong, or can an international order be built in which states will work for the common good? These were questions to which Leacock would return throughout his life but increasingly as a public intellectual rather than as an academic.

# CHAPTER SEVEN

# The Public Intellectual

Leacock was too restless, his range of interests too wide, and his attitudes toward universities too ambivalent for him to remain content with being primarily a professor. Moreover, as his national and international reputation grew, he received repeated invitations to take part in public affairs. Leacock believed in being involved in his own society, but on his own terms. He was not cut out to be part of a team and he knew it. He usually refused requests to serve on committees or advisory boards; his service on an electoral reform commission in Quebec in 1911 was a rare exception. The Conservative Party repeatedly asked him to stand as a candidate; he repeatedly refused. (He always claimed, though, that he would have served in the Canadian Senate if he had been asked.)

He was right in his refusals. He was temperamentally incapable of toeing the line as a good party member. Furthermore his political views, as he pointed out in *The Hohenzollerns in America,* were eclectic: "Let me say in commencing that I am a Liberal Conservative, or, if you will, a Conservative Liberal with a strong dash of sympathy with the Socialist idea, a friend of Labour, and a believer in Progressive Radicalism." His ideal political party, he wrote in the 1930s, would combine "the empire patriotism of the Conservative, the stubborn honesty of the Liberal, the optimism of the Socialist, the driving power of the Social Creditor, and the unsullied enthusiasm of all who write on their banner the name and the inspiration of youth."

He generally supported the Conservative Party and turned out in election campaigns, most often in his home Ontario riding of East Simcoe, to speak on its behalf when he felt the issues demanded it. In 1911 that meant speaking against the Liberals' reciprocity proposals and in 1935 for the solutions to the Depression being proposed by the Conservative prime minister, R.B. Bennett. (Leacock had known and liked Bennett since they had campaigned on the same side in 1911, and he also disliked the Liberal leader, William Lyon Mackenzie King, whom he saw as being dangerously hostile to the British Empire.) When Bennett was prime minister between 1930 and 1935, he consulted Leacock on ways of dealing with the Depression. Before the Imperial Conference of 1932, which was held in Ottawa, for example, Bennett sent Leacock a confidential memorandum on monetary policy for his views and a couple of years later asked for his advice in setting up the Bank of Canada. When Bennett went on the radio in 1935 to propose his own version of a New Deal for Canada, many of his ideas ran parallel to those that Leacock had been advocating. When the talks were issued as a pamphlet, Leacock wrote the introduction.

Although the term was not yet widely in use, Leacock's role was that of the public intellectual in a country which was not yet used to having them. During Leacock's lifetime, foreign visitors complained that Canada was dull and provincial. "So this is Winnipeg," said Oscar Wilde on his North American tour in the 1870s. "I can tell it's not Paris." George Bernard Shaw was no kinder in 1914: "High civilization is not compatible with the romance of the pioneer communities of Canada." The exciting intellectual and artistic developments occurred, he said, in the world's great cities, such as London or New York. This was typical metropolitan snobbishness, but it is true that Canada, with its relatively small population, could not support the arts and learning that Great Britain or the United States could. Canadian universities remained small until the Second World War and they tended to concentrate on practical learning. In 1918, for example, the University of Toronto had a total of 213 faculty in Arts and Science while Medicine alone had 193. Furthermore, Canadians tended to be conservative when it came to new ideas. Plays by writers such as George Bernard Shaw or Henrik Ibsen were staged infrequently and, when they were, greeted with derision. "Let's forget if we can," said a Winnipeg critic of a production of *Ghosts*. "The Ibsen cult may be all right but in this morally healthy western community we want none of his gruesome dissections." Although it was a prejudice that Leacock shared, he was more like Shaw and Ibsen than he admitted since he too believed in the importance of thinking about and discussing his own society.

Small as Canadian society was, Leacock and a handful of other public intellectuals—his old headmaster Sir George Parkin, for example, or his great friend Andrew Macphail—did have platforms, before the First World War mainly through print or lecturing. The urbanization of Canada and equally important the spread of education and public libraries along with higher literacy rates meant that there was a growing audience for discussions of such subjects as politics and social reform.

From his early days as a writer, Leacock had reached out to the wider audience beyond the academic world to discuss the great questions of the time. His use of humour, he firmly believed, was a valuable tool. The public, he maintained, needed to be beguiled into dealing with serious issues. "For information the reader cares nothing," he wrote in *Unsolved Riddles.* "If he absorbs it, it must be by accident and unawares." Even before the First World War, he was a public figure, writing regularly in Canadian newspapers and magazines. In 1910–11, for example, he produced the series Practical Political Economy in *Saturday Night.* The Canadian public treated his ideas seriously although, inevitably, not everyone agreed with him. Newspapers wrote editorials for and against his views. His lectures were covered as important public events; often newspapers reprinted the whole text. During the First World War, the Canadian government distributed 250,000 copies of his pamphlet "National Organization for War," an extraordinarily high number considering the total population of Canada was 8,000,000. (The equivalent today would be 1,000,000 copies.) Canadian political and business leaders consulted him frequently. When R.B. Bennett asked him to run for Parliament in 1935, his letter to Leacock said, "Your wide knowledge, your great reputation, and your disinterested approach to problems affecting the welfare of the country could not but be of the utmost value."

The other vehicle for public debate, especially before radio (the first broadcast licences were given after the First

World War) was the lecture. Increasingly, Leacock gained a reputation as an accomplished public performer. His first foray into lecturing came about by chance in 1906 when a former student invited him to talk to the Montreal meeting of the Canadian Manufacturers Association over the objections of its committee, who thought a university professor would be dull. Leacock was such a success that he was immediately invited to speak at a large Toronto meeting. It was the start of a long, profitable career which took him all over Canada, the United States, and the British Empire. By the 1920s, he was making $350 for a single lecture in the United States, an impressive sum considering that his annual salary at McGill was around $5,500.

Being Leacock, he often started with a joke. "The public," he loved to say, "is only interested in sex, murder, or, among the sophisticated, sex-murder." In fact, he took his lectures seriously. "Next time you are at a public dinner," he wrote, "notice the men at the head table who sit and eat celery by the bunch and never stop. Those are the men who are going to speak." While his wife was alive, he would ask her not to come because she made him too nervous. "No one likes lecturing," he claimed in his biography of Mark Twain, "except those who can't do it." Twain, and perhaps Leacock is talking of himself as well, felt that public lectures were demeaning, and made him into a buffoon rather than the man of letters he wanted to be.

Certainly Leacock has some pointed, and funny, things to say about the experience. Bad audiences, for example, like the one in Winnipeg that was "heavy as hell." And the experienced lecturer gets to recognize certain types: the man "with a big motionless face like a melon" who always sits near the front and never laughs; the old lady who thinks the lecture is immoral whatever the subject; or the man who leaves slowly and ostentatiously in the middle of the lecture, probably to catch his train but with the air of someone who can take no more. There is the pain of the introduction: the chairman who fumbles through his notes trying to find the speaker's name; the one who promises to be brief and goes on for half an hour; or the one who assures the audience solemnly that it is all right to laugh even if they do not feel up to it. And then there are the journalists, like the one who asks Leacock for a summary of the main points of the speech he has just given. "I didn't get to hear it," he explains. "I was at the hockey game."

Nevertheless Leacock was made for the lecture stage. He was a man of many and strong opinions on the big issues of the day: he was for the British Empire, for example, and against Canadian union with the United States, for drink and against prohibition. With his range of interests and wide reading he could speak equally confidently on universities, women, tariffs, taxes, literature, religion, humour, or great figures (generally men) of the past. He also became a very accomplished performer. Perhaps he became too good. One of his oldest friends felt that Leacock increasingly spoke with an air as if to say, "I, the great Stephen Leacock, will now delight you." That may be why his only attempt at radio broadcasting, in the mid-1930s, was such a failure; Leacock kept roaring with laughter at his own remarks.

In the years before the First World War, when Leacock first caught public attention as a leading Canadian intellectual, one of the main issues before Canadians, and Americans as well, was how to reform what many felt to be a sick society. The rapid growth of the boom years had brought prosperity, to be sure, but it had also exacerbated the gulf between the very rich and the poor. While the plutocrats of *Arcadian Adventures* and of real cities such as Toronto and Montreal lived in their mansions, the working-class slums were dark, crowded, and noisome. In *The Unsolved Riddle of Social Justice*, which he published just after the war, Leacock wrote:

> Few persons can attain to adult life without being
> profoundly impressed by the appalling inequalities

of our human lot. Riches and poverty jostle one another in our streets. The tattered outcast dozes on his bench while the chariot of the wealthy is drawn by. The palace is the neighbourhood of the slum. We are, in modern life, so used to this that we no longer see it.

People, many people, across the political spectrum, were in fact seeing it. The question was who or what was to blame and what to do about it. While the extreme left blamed capitalism itself, the mainstream in North America looked to human failings. Monopolies over utilities, for example, were gouging the ordinary people. Cities were failing the citizens and ignoring the poor because they were inefficient or corrupt or both. If things were not cleaned up, and soon, North American society ran a terrible moral danger, and if the excesses of capitalism were not brought under control, it might well face revolution as well. Progressives on both sides of the border denounced a heterogeneous group of villains from the robber barons to the big banks to the old-style ward-heeling politicians and demanded clean government and a better-regulated capitalism. As the characters in *Arcadian Adventures* remark, indignation over corruption and social misery and demands for reform were suddenly everywhere. "The thing came like a wave." Everyone suddenly realized that the city's government was quite rotten. "Look at the aldermen, they said,—rotten! Look at the city solicitor, rotten! And as for the mayor himself,—phew!"

In Canada, the reform movement was closely associated with the Protestant Church, so much so that it was commonly known as the Social Gospel. J.D. Woodsworth, later to be the first leader of the forerunner of the New Democratic Party, the Co-operative Commonwealth Federation; Nellie McClung, the crusader for women's rights; and a young Mackenzie King were all part of the movement. Leacock was not. While he sympathized with many of their aims and shared their belief that moral regeneration was the key to a healthy society, he did not share their faith that institutional reforms, new rules and regulations, and more democracy could bring about the necessary changes. Like Winston Churchill, Leacock thought that democracy was the worst form of government—except for all the others. In a speech he gave to the Empire Club in Toronto in 1907, he excoriated "the little turkey-cocks" in Ottawa who were busy feathering their own nests and not thinking of the public good. "The mud-bespattered politicians of the trade, the party men and party managers, give us in place of patriotic statecraft the sordid traffic of a tolerated jobbery."

His skepticism about both democracy and the reform movement comes out in his writings of the period. Mariposa's politics are not corrupt like those of the big cities, or so its citizens proudly say. "They might,—it's only human,—accept a job or a contract from the government, but if they did, rest assured it would be in a broad national spirit and not for the sake of the work itself. No, sir. Not for a minute." Mr. Smith, the cunning and successful hotelier, runs as a Conservative without knowing a thing about either tariff reform or imperial defence policy, the two great issues of the pre–First World War election. He wins partly because his supporters, as he instructs them, vote and keep voting all day. And, at the crucial moment, he spreads the rumour that he has been elected by an overwhelming majority and that brings out the undecided who have held back to make sure they are on the winning side. In *Arcadian Adventures,* the Clean Government Association, backed heavily it must be noted by the rich, sweeps the municipal elections as Dr. Boomer's students armed with baseball bats surround the polling booths to ensure fair play. That night there is a reception at the Mausoleum Club; as the waiters pour the champagne, the news comes that the Citizen's Light utility company has been given a franchise for two hundred years. "At the word of it, the grave faces of manly bondholders flushed with pride, and the soft eyes of listening shareholders laughed back in joy. For they had no doubt or fear, now that clean government had come. They knew what the company could do."

Leacock also parted company with the reform movement over prohibition. The banning of alcohol stood in, like abortion or same-sex marriage today, for a much wider range of issues. For the reformers, alcohol summed up everything that was corrupt about society and its prohibition was seen as both the key to and the symbol of change. Alcohol destroyed people and broke up families and it sapped the will to work. The liquor companies used their ill-got wealth to corrupt politics. Canadian opinion was divided on the issue. The Roman Catholic Church tended to oppose prohibition, which it saw as an attempt to impose Protestant values. (French Canadians saw it more as imposing English ones.) Conservatives such as Premier Rodmond Roblin in Manitoba attacked "Prohibitionist cranks and clerical politicians." In the end, the federal government of Sir Wilfrid Laurier declined to bring in countrywide prohibition, and the reformers were forced to go for local options. Much to Leacock's annoyance, Orillia voted to go dry.

Leacock objected strenuously to "the tyranny of the prohibitionist"; indeed it became something of a crusade with him. By instinct and conviction a conservative, he saw prohibition as a vicious example of the overregulation of society. By declaring people criminals for wanting a drink, it only encouraged them to break the law and real criminals to profit from the illegal sale of alcohol. Prohibition, Leacock thought, also encouraged hypocrisy. In dry areas, alcohol could be prescribed for medical conditions: "It is only necessary to go to a drugstore and lean up against the counter and make a gurgling noise like apoplexy." In *Sunshine Sketches,* the Knights of Pythias, who are dedicated to temperance, organize an outing on the *Mariposa Belle,* but there is plenty of alcohol aboard: Henry Mullins, the bank manager, carries his hip flask "as a sort of amendment to the constitution."

Leacock refused to take money for lecturing against prohibition and he declined to lecture at dry events. When the president of Bethlehem Steel asked him to talk at a dinner for the two senators from Pennsylvania, Leacock asked a friend to explain why it was out of the question: "It is utterly impossible for him to make an entertaining, mirth-provoking after-dinner talk to a prohibition gathering." He loved to claim, in what is surely an apocryphal story, that he had to cancel an expedition with the great polar explorer Vilhjalmur Stefansson when he found out that it would be dry. Being Leacock, he made humour out of prohibition. "This book," he says in *Wet Wit and Dry Humour* (1931), "is compiled in friendly appreciation of Prohibition in the United States, the greatest thing that ever happened—to Canada." The trouble is, as with other sketches where Leacock is being angry, that they are not very funny. His sketch about Mr. Pickwick's dry Christmas is dreary and "Confessions of a Soda Fiend" too sarcastic.

Leacock described himself as a liberal conservative; today he would be described as a pink Tory. He believed in progress, that human beings and human societies were gradually advancing and improving, but he was conservative in his conviction that there was much to honour and preserve in the institutions and values that society had constructed over many centuries. He was liberal or pink in accepting that change must come and that what had worked for one generation would not necessarily suit the next. He believed, though, that change worked best when it came incrementally, that it was dangerous and foolish to introduce radical changes or to sweep existing practices and institutions away altogether and try to rebuild society from scratch. When the British conquered French Canada in the eighteenth century, Leacock argued in *Baldwin, Lafontaine, Hincks,* his contribution to the Makers of Canada series, they were quite right not to introduce democratic self-government to their new subjects. It could only have ended, Leacock argued, in "chaos and disaster" because the French Canadians had lived under an autocracy and had no experience in any other form of government. Yet during the next century, the British under the influence of such statesmen as Lord Durham and Lord Elgin wisely and rightly expanded the political liberty enjoyed by the peoples of their Canadian colonies. And Canadian reformers such as Robert Baldwin in Upper Canada (now Ontario) and Louis-Hippolyte LaFontaine in Lower Canada (now Quebec) were equally wise and right in the moderation of their demands. Baldwin, says Leacock, was taunted by the Radicals such as William Lyon Mackenzie because he held fast to one key principle: that the British colonies should have responsible government, where the executive answered to an elected legislature. In fact, in Leacock's view, Baldwin and LaFontaine, his colleague in Lower Canada, were absolutely right. Once responsible government was achieved, grievances, such as excessive taxation or corruption in the government, could be dealt with and more change could gradually come. Although LaFontaine opposed the union of Upper and Lower Canada, which would leave the French at a disadvantage, he recognized that responsible government held the promise of good government and, equally important, an alliance between like-minded reformers, both French and English, which could work to the advantage of both.

Following the great nineteenth-century thinker John Stuart Mill, Leacock also believed in tempering his principles by necessity and a concern for his fellow human beings. He resisted sweeping social engineering or extensive government control, but he held strongly throughout his life that government should properly look after the common good and that society should help its less fortunate members. Like a majority of Canadians then and now, he looked for a middle way, rejecting radical individualism on the one hand and socialism on the other. "Too great an amalgamation of the individual and the state is as dangerous an ideal as a too great emancipation of the individual will," he wrote in *Elements of Political Science,* and it was a view he never changed. His objections were both moral and practical. What he described as "pure individualism" (we might call it neo-conservatism or libertarianism today) is bad for the economy because it denies the benefits of efficient government regulations and institutions and immoral because it runs counter "to the most instinctive impulses of humanity." Socialism, on the other hand, as he wrote to Montreal businessman William Massey Birks, "is a beautiful dream that can never be realized. But it invites the sympathy of many of the kindest and best minds in the world, (including my own) even when they cannot believe in it. In practice it is bound to fail." And communism, where everything is owned and managed by the state, led inevitably to tyranny.

Although Leacock accepted that change was necessary and inevitable, he did not invariably welcome it. As a product of the Victorian age, he had grown up with a faith in progress. Society was marching onward and upward. From humour to science, things were getting better. As he wrote optimistically in the first edition of *Elements of Political Science,* "It is hardly to be denied that the principle of democratic rule has now become a permanent and essential factor in political institutions and that it alone can form the basis of the state of the future." Yet when he considered the results of progress, Leacock was often nostalgic for the past, for the world of Mariposa.

He saw society changing but regretted what was being lost. Farming, for example, was becoming more efficient and businesslike. "I for one," Leacock wrote in *Hellements of Hickonomics,* "cannot bear to think that the old independent farming is to go: that the breezy call of incense breathing morn is to be replaced by the timeclock of a regimented, socialized, super-mechanical land-factory." The class he came from, the gentry who lived off inherited wealth and property but who had no idea of how to earn a living, had gone. "Perhaps we don't want them. But they had the good luck that, in their lives, money in the sense meant here, didn't enter." Worse, with the blurring of differences in society, the world was turning flat. "A queer sort of uniformity," Leacock writes in his sour little 1932 piece "L'Envoi: What Next?," "something like a great stillness, is coming over the world." Humans are being stifled, becoming less creative and innovative.

As an economist and a historian, Leacock acknowledged the huge increase in the world's productive forces which had occurred since the industrial revolution of the nineteenth century; as a conservative, he did not have to like all of its consequences. No one should be sentimental, he wrote in his *Unsolved Riddle of Social Justice,* about the centuries before the Industrial Revolution when the poor lived and died in misery. Today there was more than enough to go around and people had access to education and opportunities undreamed of in the past. Yet, as the great economic machinery churned on, it was producing more and more unnecessary things. "The basic raw materials are worked into finer and finer forms to supply new 'wants', as they are called, and to represent a vast quantity of 'satisfactions' not existing before." Yet are human beings more content with their lives than they once were? Leacock did not think so. "How, then, are we to explain this extraordinary discrepancy between human power and resulting human happiness?"

In his 1938 piece "Then and Now: Were We Happier Fifty Years Ago?" Leacock is not entirely joking when he answers yes. Life then, he says, was simpler and more satisfying. "Life was all so simple. Can you wonder that people died at thirty-five? They'd finished it." Courtship was quick and straightforward. You got married early and you made do on a small amount of money. The world and its troubles were far away. "How beautifully far away. No submarines, no air, no bombs, no gas." They had their fun and amusements back then too, better than what exists in the present. Today, says Leacock, the youngster has seen everything in the movies and is thoroughly jaded. There is nothing left for him but crime. "It is quite possible indeed that the world will swing upside down, like a revolving pyramid, with crime, the criminal class, at the top." And that was meant to be a funny piece.

The 1930s, with the Depression and the increasing turmoil in the international scene, certainly gave grounds for gloom, but Leacock's pessimism was deeply engrained. In one of his earliest writings, "The Man in Asbestos: An Allegory of the Future," which he published in his 1911

*Nonsense Novels,* he paints a grim view of the distant future. The narrator walks along the "silent, moss-grown desolation" of Broadway. There are few humans to be seen. Everything seems grey, yet surely humanity had achieved its dreams. "Here was the elimination of work, the end of hunger and cold, the cessation of the hard struggle, the downfall of change and death—nay the very millennium of happiness. And yet, somehow, there seemed something wrong with it all."

Leacock was optimistic, though, when it came to the future of Canada. He believed that it was a great country, with the potential to become even greater. The twenty-first century, he thought, would belong to Canada. What it needed though were more people, millions more—but only people of the right sort, and that meant from northern Europe. He strongly opposed Asian immigration—the "Asiatic peril"—or the mass influx of immigrants from central Europe before the First World War on the grounds that peoples such as the Chinese, Ukrainians, Poles, or Russians were not good for Canadian society. (To be fair, he changed his mind later, at least on the European immigrants, who, he wrote in his 1941 history of Canada, helped to build the West through their "energy and their industry and their new patriotism towards their new home.")

Leacock's views have an unpleasant ring today, but they were typical of the times. He believed that human races, like species, had adapted and evolved and the result had been to leave some further ahead than others. Cool climates, for example, had produced more energetic races: "The rigour of the cold," he wrote in one of his last pieces, "and the stimulus of effort bred the white races whose superiority no one must doubt." Aboriginal Canadians, though, for some reason had not responded to the challenges in the same way: "The red man would not work; he would rather die." (Never consistent, he seems not to have remembered that his favourite fishing companion, Jake Gaudaur, was an Aboriginal.) His views on blacks were, not surprisingly, equally racist. Black labourers in South Africa's mines, he wrote in 1939, needed only music and vaudeville to keep them happy. "Without that, the niggers wouldn't work, would pine away and die." In the end, all they wanted was to be able to leave with enough money "to go home and buy two wives and a spy glass and a case of gin." One of the few prejudices of his time he seems not to have shared is against Jews, which is curious given the casual and unreflecting anti-Semitism of his class and background and the notorious anti-Semitism of McGill, which in his time had formal quotas designed to limit the number of Jews. He treated his

Jewish students no differently from the others and, where he could, helped them as much. And the same Leacock who said appalling things about Aboriginals and blacks could deplore the "race hatred" ravaging Europe during the Second World War and write, in one of his last pieces: "All the people in the world, taken by and large, are mighty fine people, with energy and kindness and love, valuing just the same things that we do, with the same care for their children and their friends and their home town."

In the early part of his career, he saw Canada as very much part of the British Empire. This was not as reactionary a view as it would sound today. Ties with the British Isles were still very strong; more than 10 percent of Canada's population, according to the 1911 census, had been born there and well over half were descended from British immigrants. Canadians, especially English-speaking ones, saw themselves as British subjects who happened to live in Canada. For Leacock, Canadians' great weakness, and Canada's danger, was that they were too selfish and materialistic, too prone to fall for wild schemes to make money fast (as his own uncle had in the 1880s). The British Empire counteracted those tendencies by lifting Canadians out of their own self-interested and materialistic preoccupations. "This is our need, our supreme need of the Empire," he wrote in 1907,

"—not for its ships and guns, but for the greatness of it, the soul of it, aye for the very danger of it."

Moreover, being part of the British Empire, certainly until the interwar years, meant that Canada was part of the world's leading power. Membership in the Empire gave Canada and Canadians a status they could not have had on their own, and, as important in those days, protection against their great neighbour to the south. For all his preference for freer trade, Leacock campaigned in 1911 against Sir Wilfrid Laurier's proposals for greater reciprocity with the United States on the grounds that it would lead Canada into too close a union with the U.S.

Like many Canadians, then and now, Leacock had ambivalent views on the United States. He admired its writers such as Mark Twain and Robert Benchley and its statesmen such as President Lincoln. He disliked its outbursts of religiosity and, of course, strongly disapproved of its adoption of prohibition. He did not want Canada to become part of the United States, but he felt he was somehow part of the American family. He did not want to move back to Britain, he wrote in his moving "I'll Stay in Canada," partly because he would be too far away from Americans. "You see, with us it's second nature, part of our lives, to be near them." We Canadians go there, he told his imaginary British audience, and they come to Canada. Their colleges and clubs are just like Canadian ones. "Honestly, you can't tell where you are unless you happen to get into a British Empire Society; and anyway, they have those in Boston and in Providence, and the Daughters of the American Revolution is practically a British organization—so all that is fifty-fifty."

In the years before the First World War, Leacock spoke and wrote strongly in favour of a reinvigorated British Empire, with a strong government with representation from the Empire. It was a common complaint at the time from the British colonies that they were expected to support policies made in Britain and fight in British wars, yet they had no representation. The time, said Leacock in a 1907 pamphlet, had come for Canadians to stop whining and demand full membership in a permanent and indivisible Empire. The model he had in mind was a federation, like Canada, where the so-called White Dominions (Australia, Canada, New Zealand, and, later, South Africa) would run their own affairs, but where there might be an imperial cabinet, imperial legislature, and imperial bureaucracy to deal with issues which affected the whole. How that would work in practice given the vast distances and the relatively slow communications of the time and where parts of the Empire in Asia and Africa would fit in were not things that the supporters of imperial federation ever solved. Leacock himself was never all that precise about what he envisaged. He ought to have, said one of his critics in exasperation, "some conception of what it is he is preaching about—some notion, vague or otherwise, of what it is he wants us to do."

His advocacy of a stronger Empire was to Leacock completely compatible with his loyalty to Canada. Like many imperialists, including Sir Robert Borden, the Conservative prime minister from 1911 to 1920, Leacock wanted an independent Canada within a strong British Empire. They were moved not so much by deference to Britain—British incompetence in the Boer War and then in the early stages of the First World War helped to take care of that—but by a conviction that Canada had something useful to contribute. He was an imperialist, Leacock wrote firmly in this period, because he did not want to be a colonial any longer. "This Colonial status is a worn-out, by-gone thing. The sense and feeling of it has become harmful to us. It limits the ideas and circumscribes the patriotism of our people." What Leacock and others like him could not fully grasp was that by pushing for greater power within the Empire, they were in the longer run undermining it.

In Britain, Canada, and the other Dominions, there were imperial federation leagues and committees. A Round Table movement of bright young men toured the Empire before the First World War to stir up, like King Arthur's knights, enthusiasm for the holy grail of Empire unity and set up local Round Tables. Leacock belonged to the Montreal one, although it is not clear how active he was, and he was friendly with other Canadian Round Table supporters such as Sir George Parkin, who had been his headmaster when he was a student at Upper Canada College.

In 1907 Leacock got an offer which neither he nor McGill were inclined to refuse. Earl Grey, the Governor General and a strong supporter of the Round Table Movement, invited him to tour the Empire lecturing on imperial unity. Although he later made fun of himself ("These lectures were followed almost immediately by the Union of South Africa, the Banana Riots in Trinidad, and the Turko-Italian war...."), Leacock undertook his mission with a strong sense of responsibility. "I should aim," he wrote to Grey, "at capturing the interest of the leading minds of the community." He would not indulge in polemics, Leacock went on, "But there might be and ought to be, nevertheless, a guiding thread of thought,—a presentation of the growth and meaning of imperial unity, an appeal for earnest and intelligent co-operation in the future problems of the Empire."

Leacock and his wife were away for almost a year. Their first stop was England, where they were made much of by leading British imperialists. Leacock stayed with Rudyard Kipling and lunched with Arthur Balfour, recently the Conservative prime minister. Everyone, Leacock wrote to his mother, was very nice to him—"no doubt would forget me tomorrow." He put some backs up, though, with a humorous article in the *Morning Post,* which compared the Empire to a farm. The sons (the Dominions such as Canada and Australia) were getting fed up with their father (Britain), who was set in his ways. "The old man's got old and he don't know it." The energetic younger men were going to have to get together and take over. A young Winston Churchill called the article "offensive twaddle." Leacock was echoing a mood, though, which was becoming increasingly common in the Dominions as their sense of nationhood and pride grew. The Boer War, fought only a few years before between the Afrikaner farmers in South Africa and the British Empire, had brought Australians, Canadians, and New Zealanders flocking to Britain's aid, but it had also shaken the Dominions' faith in British competence and leadership.

From England the Leacocks went on to Paris, where an already travel-weary Leacock complained to his mother that he would much rather be at the lake. "Paris is very lovely but

Orillia is much livelier (joke for George [his brother]).ʺ From Paris they went to Marseilles to catch the boat which would take them through the Suez Canal and on to Australia and then to New Zealand and South Africa. "Being on board ship is mere damn foolishness," Leacock wrote home, but he consoled himself with thoughts of the house he was going to build on Lake Couchiching when he got back to Canada. Although he had not enjoyed the travelling, did not like the Australians, and disapproved strongly of the English for starting the Boer War—"a huge crime from start to finish, organised and engineered by a group of plutocrats and tyrants"—Leacock returned from his trip as firm an imperialist as ever.

When the First World War broke out, Leacock at once rallied to the cause. Although he was too old to fight, he took on a heavy round of lecturing to raise money for the Belgians, whose country had been occupied and plundered by the Germans. Like many of his fellow Canadians, he was highly critical of the United States for staying out of the war in its first years. In *Further Foolishness,* published in 1916, he satirizes pacifists and neutralists such as Norman Angell, the well-known English journalist, and William Jennings Bryan, who had just resigned as U.S. Secretary of State. Not only are they foolish, they are, even worse, teetotallers. Woodrow

Wilson, the American president, appears as a booby, sitting in the White House and telling himself how beautiful the world is. Every so often he writes a note to protest the latest German atrocity, but when the Germans produce increasingly feeble excuses, accepts them at once. In 1917, when the United States entered the war against Germany, Leacock was delighted. "I knew," he wrote in a sketch in which New York's Father Knickerbocker abandons his nightclubs and carousing at the sound of distant guns, "that a great nation had cast aside the bonds of sloth and luxury, and was girding itself to join in the fight for the free democracy of mankind."

His surviving letters, however, show a Leacock whose life went on during the war years with few changes and who remained somewhat detached from the fighting in Europe. His letters tend to be about his own concerns, his latest work, for example, or his finances. They also talk about a momentous event in 1915—the birth of his first child, his son Stephen. Decades later, Leacock wrote to his beloved niece Barbara as she was expecting her first child, "Whatever you get you will wonder that you could ever have wanted the other … I spent months in dreaming of a daughter, and forgot it in one minute & couldnt even understand it." Leacock and his wife, Beatrix, had been married for fifteen years and so the arrival of Stephen was an unexpected gift.

Leacock wrote an ecstatic letter to his mother: "I never yet saw a baby that looked so complete, so all there, so little like a red monkey as Stephen does." The child was going to be both Leacock's joy and his cross.

# CHAPTER EIGHT

# Life between Two Wars

Like many of his contemporaries in Canada and the other Western democracies, Leacock greeted the end of the war in November 1918 with cautious relief. He watched the establishment of the League of Nations, which was supposed to provide collective security for its members against aggression and work for the common good of the world, with a measure of hope mixed with skepticism. The league, so Leacock argued, could settle disputes among nations if the parties agreed, but it could not provide protection against what he called "pirate nations" (today we prefer "rogue states"). In the end, he felt, and he was by no means alone, that the only safety for a nation lay in having strong military forces. And, he believed, that would remain the case as long as the world was divided up into nation states. In the 1920 edition of his *Elements of Political Science,* he warned: "The wider prospect of cosmopolitan union must still remain little more than a vision, an inspiration, doubtless, but worse than useless as a reliance against danger."

Although Leacock's personal life and career appeared to be going well at the start of the 1920s, the huge damage and the waste of the Great War (as it was known until another, even more destructive one came along) left him, as it did so many, despondent about the state of the world. In a dark piece, "Merry Christmas," which he wrote in 1917, Leacock has Santa Claus appealing to Father Time to look after the children harmed in the war: "I hear them everywhere—they come to me in every wind—and I see them as I wander in the night and storm—my children torn and dying in the trenches—beaten into the ground—I hear them crying from the hospitals...."

In the war's aftermath, great empires—Russia, Austria-Hungary, and Ottoman Turkey—collapsed. A score of small wars broke out in the years after 1918 as old and new nations squabbled over the spoils. Western civilization itself had been shaken, many feared, or even hoped, fatally. And there was impatience with the old order which had brought the catastrophe of the Great War and now seemed unable to cope with the challenges of the peace. Soldiers demanded jobs and houses, women the vote, and the working classes a fairer society. Social unrest, spurred on by the Bolshevik revolution in Russia, brought strikes and demonstrations, often violent ones, across Europe and North America, and the authorities cracked down, sometimes with equal violence. In

Canada, Winnipeg was paralyzed by a general strike and several demonstrators were killed by police gunfire. Leacock feared what he called a "National Hysteria" or social panic, where reasonable people abandoned the middle ground and saw issues in black or in white.

Leacock deplored revolution, but he admitted that there was much wrong with his own society. He worried that the ruling classes were failing to deal with the grave social and economic problems nations such as Canada were facing. Labour and capital were at war with each other. Wages and prices were being forced up and there was a danger that industry would come to a stop. Governments, already deeply in debt because of the war, were printing money and spending it in a delirium. The malign influence of Bolshevism was infecting Western civilization. Reforms, he was convinced, must come if society were not to disintegrate. For all his gloom, Leacock was surprisingly optimistic about the possibility of change. The war, he felt, had shown that peoples like his fellow Canadians could pull together when they had to. "This is the supreme meaning of the war to us," he wrote in 1917. "It is the glad cry of a people that have found themselves."

In 1919 he wrote a series of articles in *The New York Times,* which came out in book form the following year as

*The Unsolved Riddle of Social Justice.* Leacock painted a lurid picture of a world on the edge of the abyss. "If we do not mend the machine," he warned, "there are forces moving in the world that will break it. The blind Samson of labour will seize upon the pillars of society and bring them down in a common destruction." After such a dramatic warning, his solutions are something of an anti-climax. People must have jobs; if there is no other way the government must provide them. Leacock adds a word of caution: the wages for jobs supplied by the government must be kept low enough that the unemployed turn to them only as a last resort. (The suggestion and the caveat are a foreshadowing of the debates around prescriptions for the Depression.) Second, those who cannot work because of illness or age must be looked after. "There is no need," says Leacock breezily, "to discuss the particular way in which this policy can best be carried out." Third, children must be given a proper start with adequate care and education. "No society is properly organized until every child that is born into it shall have an opportunity in life."

His main solution was a change of heart in his fellow Canadians. He urged them to work together and to make reforms because it was the right thing to do. He called for new approaches and a new morality, but what he really meant was that Canadians should recover the old virtues of decency, patriotism, and self-sacrifice, the very ones which they had demonstrated during the war. The world, he complains, has lost its taste "for the honest drudgery of work." People want to work less yet consume more. Public institutions did not work because those who ran them were shortsighted and, too often, venal. Unconsciously, perhaps, he was drawing on his classical education; he sounded like Cato calling the Romans to be true to the austere values of the Roman Republic.

Leacock had a special message for the upper classes. He had always been ambivalent about wealth. In *Arcadian Adventures,* he satirizes the rich as heartless, idle, and selfish, yet many of his friends and acquaintances such as Sir Edward Beatty, the president of the Canadian Pacific Railway, were among their number. He believed, or perhaps rather he hoped, that such people could also change and take on responsibility for righting the manifest wrongs in society. It was a theme he returned to frequently throughout his life. Look at the city, he said in his history of Montreal, which he published in 1942, "so beautiful in its leafy residential streets, so inspiring in its college area, so triumphant in its downtown section jostling with wealth and luxury, ostentatious with plate glass—does it not contain, like all its sister cities, those tangled, narrower streets of the part of the city where the poor live...." It was wrong that the children of the poor should live in such places, with so little hope for the future. The rich must do something; they are the only ones who can.

For Leacock, in the end, the only thing that made society better was better people. "There is," he wrote in *Montreal,* "in short, no virtue in democracy of any sort unless it carries with it the spirit of righteousness. All government comes to that." Typically, he did not put much faith in his own prescription. Human progress was slow and fitful. The question he asked in *Unsolved Riddle* about government in a socialist system expressed his skepticism about democracy as well. "Who can deny that under such a system the man with the glib tongue and persuasive manner, the babbling talker and the scheming organizer, would secure all the places of power and profit, while patient merit went to the wall."

The world did not in fact come to an end in the early 1920s and, for a time at least, societies appeared to be recovering from the Great War and the turmoil that had followed it. Leacock's own life went on in its usual fashion. He continued to produce at least a book a year, and he and Beatrix and little Stephen continued to move between Montreal and Orillia, with occasional trips farther afield, such as Leacock's lecturing tour to England in 1921. Part of the purpose of the trip was also to consult specialists because it had become clear that there was something wrong with the child whose arrival Leacock had greeted with such joy.

Little Stevie, as he came to be known, was often sick as an infant, and at some point it became apparent that he was not growing properly. If he was not a midget, he was close to one; fully-grown he was well under five feet tall. The Leacocks spared no expense and effort to find the best doctors. In England they made a special trip to Liverpool to see a famous pediatrician. Leacock's letters to Stevie's Montreal specialist, Dr. Alton Goldbloom, show his longing that the boy can be treated successfully. "I think he's growing," he said in one letter, but then added in the next breath, "But I hate to measure him." As one friend said, if Leacock had been right every time he said Stevie had grown an inch or two, the boy would have become a normal-sized adult. One of the reasons why Leacock wrote so hastily and sometimes so carelessly, so his friends thought, was his obsession with providing for his son. His worry also led him into a long and ultimately unsuccessful wrangle with Beatrix's mother as he tried to persuade her not to spend all of her share in Sir Henry Pellatt's estate but keep it in trust for her grandson, Stevie.

In 1924 Leacock suffered an even greater blow when Beatrix fell ill with breast cancer. She had been feeling under the weather for some time, and Leacock took her and Stevie to Nassau for Christmas. When he went back to McGill for his classes, he left them there for the winter. By the spring of 1925, Beatrix was still not feeling well and was obliged to cancel her social engagements. A summer in Orillia brought no improvement, and the cancer was finally diagnosed in the autumn. An operation did not help and Leacock, in desperation, decided to take her to England to see a leading expert. His friend Sir Edward Beatty used his position as president of the Canadian Pacific Railway to arrange for a special private infirmary with nurses to be set up onboard one of the CPR's liners. Beatrix was by now very weak; she died in hospital in Liverpool just before Christmas. She was forty-five years old and Leacock was fifty-five. Leacock buried her ashes in the St. Jamestown cemetery in Toronto and there they remain, although he always intended to move her to the Leacock plot at Sibbald Point on Lake Simcoe.

He never discussed his loss. That would not have been his style. For two years, though, he stayed away from his summer house and he wrote very little. He devoted considerable time and money to supporting the search for a cure for cancer, as he was to do for the rest of his life. In his writings after Beatrix's death, he occasionally refers wistfully to love and marriage. In one of the last pieces he published, he was perhaps thinking of himself when he talked of husbands who snapped and snarled at their wives but never said how much they loved them—until it was too late. In "The Transit of Venus," one of Leacock's few relatively serious short stories, a timid professor falls in love, he assumes hopelessly, with the beauty in class. His heart breaks when he thinks that she is about to marry a fellow student. It ends happily though when Professor Kitter learns that he is mistaken, and he and the golden-haired Miss Taylor walk under the elm trees and realize that they love each other. "Miss Taylor is now Mrs Arthur Lancelot Kitter, and attends college teas, and reads little papers on Chinese Philosophy at the Concordia Sigma Phi Society—and in fact, acts and behaves much as any other professor's wife."

Leacock never married again, but he developed an intense romantic friendship with an old friend and neighbour from Old Brewery Bay. Fitz Shaw, who had been a friend of Beatrix Leacock, was, like her, very pretty and vivacious and came from a good family. Those who did not much care for her said she was too fond of flirting with handsome young men and that she loved to be the centre of attention. She and Leacock became inseparable, travelling together, entertaining together, and popping in and out of each other's houses. Her husband, a Montreal businessman, seems to have increasingly led his own life. Did she and Leacock sleep together? There was gossip of course that they were having an affair. We will never know and it does not really matter. What is important is that she gave Leacock an intimate and loving friendship. His letters to her are freer and more affectionate than any of the others that have survived. (None of his to Beatrix have been found.) When he went on a long lecture tour of the Canadian west at the end of 1936, he wrote to her virtually every day. "I got 3 letters all together," he wrote from Edmonton. "Just think of it! It seemed like being home again." And from Victoria as he is about to head back East, "I'll be so glad to see you,—even to hear you."

The other increasingly important presence in his life was his niece Barbara. She came to live with him in 1927 partly as his assistant and housekeeper but also as a companion for Stevie. In turn Leacock paid her way through university and gave her a generous allowance. She stayed with him for ten years, until she married. Leacock arranged the whole wedding on the lawn at Old Brewery Bay, building an arbour and tables himself and laying in quantities of champagne, which he hated. In his usual careless fashion, he never bothered to take everything down, and the awnings sagged and the arbour eventually fell over. Barbara came back frequently to visit, and Leacock was always delighted and full of plans.

For all his personal setbacks in the 1920s, Leacock's career continued to flourish. He picked up his old routines again and more collections of his humour appeared. At the end of the 1920s, he found himself dealing with more serious subjects again. The world's economy was in trouble; excessive lending and feverish speculation combined with ineffective regulation had led to a series of bank failures and a sharp drop in the world's trade and production. The Great Depression, which started in the latter part of 1929, hit many countries, some of them, like Canada, more harshly than others. By 1932 one-quarter of the Canadian workforce was unemployed and factories and plants were standing idle. Leacock's own finances suffered; his investments lost part of their value at a time when his income from his writing and lecturing was also going down. As he recognized, though, he was one of the lucky ones. As an engaged intellectual, he set himself to search for remedies.

The fears for the future of society which he had felt at the end of the Great War came back in force. Leacock was by no means alone; capitalism had apparently collapsed and governments appeared to be incapable of dealing with the challenges they faced. The times led many voters and their political elites to search for radical solutions, whether on the left or the right. In some countries, Germany for example, politics polarized as the Nazis and the communists gained millions of new adherents. In Canada the divisions were less stark, but new political movements appeared, such as the populist Social Credit and the left-leaning Co-operative Commonwealth Federation (CCF), forerunner of the New Democratic Party. Leacock typically looked for a middle way. He thought Social Credit, with its hostility to banks and its cure-all policy of issuing money to consumers to get the economy going again, absurd. "It means voting for Jesus," he wrote to his niece Barbara. There was no sound economic basis in it at all, just the slogan of "The plain honest people against the money oppressors...." As for the CCF, in Leacock's view it was heading down the slippery slope toward socialism.

Politically Leacock supported an old friend, R.B. Bennett, the federal Conservative leader and prime minister from 1930 to 1935, as he tried to balance between the need to provide relief for the poor and the poorest provinces and keep government expenditure under control. And when, at the start of 1935, Bennett made a series of radio speeches proposing a Canadian version of Franklin Delano

Roosevelt's New Deal to get Canadians back to work, Leacock wrote the foreword to the printed version.

His own solutions for the Depression had helped Bennett to formulate his thinking. They largely echoed what Leacock had already said at the end of the war. Neither of the extremes of individualism or socialism would bring stability and prosperity to society. What was needed was a combination of government intervention and moral regeneration. Canadians needed to regain the old virtues of "Law and order, property, industry, honesty." The state, he wrote in his 1933 pamphlet, immodestly titled *Stephen Leacock's Plan to Relieve the Depression in 6 Days, To Remove It in 6 Months, To Eradicate It in 6 Years,* must undertake a huge program of public works and work with other governments to restore international trade in part by lowering the high tariff walls which nations had thrown up in a vain attempt to protect their own industries. In his 1930 book, *Economic Prosperity in the British Empire,* he also supported measures to integrate the separate economies of the British Empire so that at least there trade could flourish.

As before, too, he sounded the alarm—the Depression, he said in 1933, might be the last one before civilization collapsed—but he also refused to offer comprehensive or radical solutions. At times he was maddeningly vague. We cannot, he told his fellow economists in 1934, leave the economy to be run by the unrestrained forces of individual choice and the free market. What was needed was not laissez-faire but, as he put it in bad French, faire-faire, "not let things happen but 'make things happen.'" But, he added hastily, he was not advocating socialism, which could not work. Frank Underhill, a rising young historian and considerably to the left of Leacock, said unkindly, "Professor Stephen Leacock still remains our leading humorist when it comes to writing serious books about Canadian social problems."

The Depression further reinforced, if they needed reinforcing, Leacock's prejudices against his own profession. Economics, he said in his 1934 talk, which he then published as "What Is Left of Adam Smith?" was completely useless as a discipline. It is like a bankrupt still claiming that it has wonderful assets. "It cites a wilderness, not of opinion, but of statistics and facts, all apparently bearing on nothing, gets confused, breaks down and cries—a very picture of senile collapse." The Depression also renewed Leacock's skepticism about democracy. In 1934 he told the Canadian Political Science Association that modern society was getting too complex to be run by political parties. The system itself was deeply flawed. Politicians busied themselves with making alliances or engaging in fictitious opposition to each other, but that only concealed their own inadequacies. What was needed, he said, were good men "trained and specialized to carry on the government." This sounds suspiciously like the efficiencies being promised at the time by authoritarian governments of both the right and the left, but what Leacock seems to have been thinking of is something more like Plato's Guardians, who put the common good above all else.

# CHAPTER NINE

# The Melancholy Twilight

While he was engaged in the public discussion of the Depression, Leacock managed to find time to write a biography of Mark Twain (published in 1932) and two years later one of Charles Dickens. The collections of humour continued to come out as well, three alone in 1936. He went on accumulating honours, an honorary degree from the University of Michigan and, in 1935, the Mark Twain Medal of Honour, joining a distinguished and also eclectic list which included General John Pershing, Benito Mussolini, Rudyard Kipling, Franklin Delano Roosevelt, and Willa Cather.

Nevertheless, his books were not selling as well as they had once done and reviewers suggested that perhaps he was getting stale. Leacock complained vociferously about his falling income, yet he still managed to make at least twice his university salary every year and keep up his two houses. He worried about his finances partly because of his son but also because his family, whom he had always supported generously, frequently needed his help. His brother Charlie was becoming increasingly eccentric and incapable of looking after himself; Leacock repeatedly advanced him money and paid his bills.

In 1934 Leacock's mother died. The family gathered on a cold, clear winter day to bury her in the family plot beside Lake Simcoe. "It did not seem sad at the time," Leacock wrote later to friends, "but now it seems so strange & sad all the time to think that she is gone." He lost another old friend at the same time when Sir Arthur Currie, the principal of McGill, died. Currie had admired and protected Leacock; his successor was not going to be as accommodating.

Sadly, Leacock's relationship with his son was proving difficult. Leacock was surely partly to blame as he veered between trying to toughen Stevie up and being overprotective. A friend remembers him at Old Brewery Bay snapping at a young Stevie: "For heaven's sake take a bath—you smell worse than the dogs," but he would also spend time writing plays for his son and arranging playmates for him. By the time Stevie went to McGill in 1936, Leacock had retired, but he continued to spend the winters in Montreal so that he could keep an eye on his son's education. He treated little Stevie, as everyone tended to call him, as a child long after the boy had grown up. Stevie bitterly resented this, as well as his own physical problems. He was intelligent and did well at university. Even as an undergraduate, though, there were signs of the troubles to come. He drank and smoked to excess, to the point where the University Club banned him. There is a curious and sad story that when Stevie graduated in 1940, Leacock dressed up for the ceremony but could not bring himself to attend, staying in the University Club instead. "Oh, to hell with it," he said when someone asked him about his decision. "People would say who is that funny old man in the shabby clothes and answer the funny old man was Stephen Leacock and that he was probably drunk."

In 1936 Leacock suffered a major blow when he was obliged to retire from McGill. The university had recently adopted a policy of mandatory retirement at sixty-five, although the board had the ability to make exceptions. The new president, A.E. Morgan, a British academic, was not prepared to make such a recommendation in Leacock's case and he was probably right. Leacock may have been an ornament to the university, but he had long since ceased to keep up in his own field and he had largely left the management of his department to his subordinates. Leacock was deeply hurt and very angry. "I have plenty to say about the Governors of McGill putting me out of the university," he told the newspapers. "But I have all eternity to say it in. I shall shout it down to them." And shout he did. He was part of the notorious Senility Gang, he told his readers, convicted by a heartless university administration. His speech at a farewell dinner at the Ritz in the spring of 1936 was entitled "Paradise Lost," and for Leacock that was no exaggeration. He never reconciled himself to being outside the charmed university world. "I'd say the sparkle had gone out of him," said his former student Carl Goldenberg.

Retirement, to Leacock, was bleak. In his 1939 *Too Much College,* he wrote:

> Listen, it's like this. Have you ever been out for a late autumn walk in the closing part of the afternoon, and suddenly looked up to realize that the leaves have practically gone? You hadn't realized it. And you notice that the sun has set already, the day gone before you knew it—and with that a cold wind blows across the landscape. That's retirement.

Moreover he hated growing old. "More nonsense and guff has been talked about old age than of any other time of life."

There were compensations of course. He remained much in demand, as a humorist, a thinker, and a lecturer. In the fall after his retirement, he and Stevie, who had been taken out of McGill for a few weeks, set off on an extended lecture tour of western Canada. With his usual attention to detail, Leacock sent ahead information about himself to newspaper editors. "It is far better," he said smugly, "to write one's own interviews." He used his standard repertoire of lectures, from humour to education to international relations. Because he was in the West, where local feeling and resentment of Ottawa ran high during the Depression, he also attacked regionalism. "The provinces," he wrote to a newspaper editor in England, "have turned into little kingdoms." They fight each other, setting up barriers to interprovincial trade, for example, as well as the federal government. Soon, Leacock complained, the latter will be no more than a weather bureau. Leacock wrote a series of articles which he then turned into a book called *My Discovery of the West*. A series of reflections, mixed with bits of potted history, it is not one of his best books, but in 1937 it won the new Governor General's Literary Award for Non-fiction.

What comes through clearly in the book is Leacock's abiding love of Canada. Yes, he was critical of its provincialism and regionalism and of what he saw as the selfish and short-sighted attitude of his fellow Canadians. We all grab for government money, he wrote. "Worse than that, if one may say it very gently, in dealing with government money we are individually not just quite exactly what you'd call honest." But Canada was his home. After his retirement, when an English editor asked him why he did not now come home to his birthplace, England, Leacock's reply was heartfelt. "I'll Stay in Canada," which he published in 1936, is one of his best pieces. He was indelibly Canadian, he said. His language was quite different; where the English said "Yes," he said "Yep." His manners were Canadian, not English. And Canada does not have a proper class system. "Personally I can go fishing with a taxi driver and a Toronto surgeon and an American tourist and the 'feller that rents the boat' and can't see any difference. Neither can they. There isn't any."

Canada, he goes on, has been such an exciting place with its rapid development and great future. "In the last sixty years—since I've known it—we have filled it in and filled it in like a huge picture lying in a frame from the frozen seas to the American line, from Nova Scotia to the Pacific." He loves Canada's distances and its isolation and its climate. Why would he leave all this for the turbulence of old Europe? "No thank you, Mother England. I'm 'home' now. Fetch me my carpet slippers from the farm. I'll rock it out to sleep right here."

When Samuel Bronfman asked him in 1940 to write a book on Canada for the giant Seagram's distillery firm as part of its war effort, Leacock jumped at the opportunity. The book, he said, "should show in its foreground, the passing lights and shadows of romantic history, the adventure, the exploration, the long years of conflict in arms, that make up our wonderful history of Canada; but behind all this the truer and deeper colours of the background would reflect the life of the people, the brave adversity of their pioneer days, and their gradual emergence into the plentitude of our industrial power."

In this book, as in all his writings on Canada, Leacock had something of a blind spot when it came to the French. He romanticized the great French explorers, the fur traders, or the simple habitants, but he was uncomfortable with modern French-Canadian culture and nationalism. In his book on Montreal, he has very little to say about the French presence in the city. (He also said virtually nothing about the Jews.) Despite the fact that he spoke excellent French, he moved almost exclusively in English-speaking circles. Yet he liked to maintain that one of the most important and distinctive features of Canada's development as a nation was the "real and organic unity of the two races" happily united under the British Crown. By the 1930s, he was forced to realize French-Canadian nationalists did not see it the same way. He was startled by the demands for a separate country and ridiculed the idea. "In this dream world the Government is all by orators—young orators—and they talk and talk, and fall asleep and wake up and talk." Yet he sadly concluded that the old dream of two cultures living happily together was dead, "like a beautiful landscape, now a deserted garden."

By the 1930s he was obliged to admit that his dreams of a strong, independent Canada within a strong and united British Empire were also dead. He had been wrong to support imperial unity, Leacock said in "Canada and the Monarchy," which he published in the *Atlantic Monthly* in 1939. The First World War had given increased self-confidence and a greater sense of nationhood to the Dominions. Canada and Canadians were no longer willing to submerge themselves in a greater British Empire. Canada and the other Dominions had signed the Treaty of Versailles at the end of the war in their own right and had joined the League of Nations as separate countries. The British Empire had drifted apart. In 1931 the Statute of Westminster had recognized that the Dominions were autonomous and no longer subordinate to Britain. What linked them now was merely a shared allegiance to the Crown and membership in the Empire, or, as it was increasingly being called, "the British Commonwealth of Nations." By 1939, so Leacock believed, the true strength of the Empire was manifesting itself in another way. It was joined by bonds of culture, affection, and deeply shared values such as liberty and democracy. More formal ties were unneeded and indeed they could be counterproductive. "They invite," he wrote in *Our British Empire,* which he published in 1940, "a grudging dispensation of assistance, a measured allotment of goodwill." An imperial federation without goodwill, he went on, "is just a chain, weak as its weakest link, and an axis a weather-cock, turning with every wind."

In such a grouping, Leacock wrote a year later, there was room too for the United States.

> The world needs a standard to which all honest men may rally, a barrier to shelter the weak against iniquity. As the keystones for such an arch, the government of free men that arose in Saxon England, and became in America government by the people and for the people, will have fulfilled its final purpose.

If the United States and Britain could pull together in the face of the challenges facing them, they could bring an enduring peace to the world. And in that partnership Canada would be "the middle term," a bridge between the U.S. and the British Empire.

Leacock remained busy after his retirement, but his letters reveal him struggling against loneliness and depression. "I had such a bad time for 2 nights that I nearly telegraphed & telephoned you," he wrote to Fitz Shaw just before Christmas in 1938. "I know it is only broken nerves & imagination & I am doing all I can—but mental illness is hard to fight." His health is deteriorating and more and more he has trouble sleeping. "I drop back into fears & abysses so easily that the only plan is to keep fighting against it," he writes to Fitz the following spring. Leacock's old friends were dying off, and, in Montreal, he increasingly looked for companionship in the University Club. His house, especially once Stevie had graduated from McGill, was too big for him; in 1939 he closed it up and moved into the Windsor Hotel.

As he had done throughout his son's life, Leacock continued to hope against all evidence that his physical condition was improving. "He has slowly grown past five feet by a fraction," the anxious father wrote to an old friend, "& is getting broader & stronger so that soon he won't have to think about his size." In reality Stevie continued to be a worry for Leacock. His son refused to take work seriously; after all, he told Carl Goldenberg, his father had left him well provided for. Leacock repeatedly tried to find his son jobs and, when Stevie made desultory attempts at writing, even trying his hand at humour, contacted publishers on his behalf. To his friends and family, Leacock spoke proudly of his son's efforts, but occasionally he flagged. Stevie was looking for a new position in Toronto, he wrote to Fitz Shaw in 1943. "I don't know what will come of that." Leacock wrote to the editor of *Maclean's* to recommend his son: "He has an unusual talent for writing smooth attractive prose and has done well with random short stories and sketches." In one of his later pieces, though, Leacock sounded a sad note about those who have only one child and no grandchildren to comfort their old age. Among the last words he said to an old friend before he died were "Look after little Stevie, look after Stephen if you can." No one, it turned out, could, and without his father to watch over him, Stevie came off the rails. He spent his last years as the town drunk in Orillia and then the even smaller town of Beaverton, running through the money his father had so carefully laid by for him.

As his life moved into its final stage, Leacock could take little comfort in the domestic and international scene in the late 1930s. Canada was recovering with painful slowness from the Depression. By 1938 national output had still not risen to where it had been in 1929. Some 16 percent of Canadians were still unemployed. The provinces continued to wrangle with one another and with the federal government. Internationally, things looked no better. The Depression had made every country look out for itself. It was a virus, said Leacock in the *Hellements of Hickonomics:* "It has put us back, centuries back, into the poisonous attitude of regarding other nations' ruin as our own welfare, and other nations' welfare as our ruin." The democracies were divided and ineffective in the face of the aggression of a Nazi Germany, a fascist Italy, or a militaristic Japan. The League of Nations was useless too; it had no more cohesion, said Leacock scornfully, "than a pyramid of billiard balls, no bond of more than a rope of sand." Do not think, he warned his fellow North Americans, that they could escape the coming conflict. "If it comes it will spread like a plague, driving across the continent with all the evil winds of disaster behind it."

The conflict did come, in the fall of 1939. "The war, the war, the war," he wrote to Fitz Shaw that September, "what we have all got to do is to keep busy doing something." Leacock hoped that he might be able to help out by teaching at McGill, but the call never came. Instead he decided that the best thing he could do was to explain to his readers, whether Canadian, British, or American, what the stakes were and why it was necessary to keep on fighting. He argued, too, as he had done at the end of the First World War, that when the war ended, the democracies must make reforms. Their people deserved it. "Our people," he wrote proudly in his history of Canada, "through all the minor divisions of race or province or social class, preserved certain ideals, stood firm on certain ground."

Leacock was nearly seventy when the war started, but he worked indefatigably to turn out his books on Canada and Montreal as well as *The British Empire* in 1940 and *Our Heritage of Liberty* in 1942. In "All Right Mr. Roosevelt," a pamphlet written in 1939 before the United States had come into the war, he avoided blaming the U.S. for its neutrality but urged Canadians and Americans to remember their great friendship. Somehow he still found the time and the capacity to write humorous sketches. In 1942 he published "My Remarkable Uncle," one of his finest pieces. Uncle Edward, E.P., swept into the Leacocks' isolated Ontario farm, bringing the glamour of the great outside world. "When we asked, 'Uncle Edward, do you know the Prince of Wales?' he answered, 'Quite intimately'—with no further explanation. It was a trick he had." The unfailingly optimistic E.P. also had the ability to sketch out great and wonderful schemes and plans, and sometimes they worked. He hit Winnipeg in the 1880s just as it was booming and in no time had become a leading political and business figure. When the crash came, E.P. carried on living in great style. He never considered his unpaid bills as dishonest; they were simply deferred. One day, he told his creditors, he expected good news from Africa, or perhaps it was China. "All his grand schemes were as open as sunlight—and as empty."

Work for Leacock had always been a refuge, and there was much to take refuge from. In the first two years of the war the news was almost unrelentingly bad. France fell with astonishing rapidity in the summer of 1940. Leacock's old friend René du Roure, who had tried to enlist in the French army even though he was well over age, drank himself to death at the news. Britain fought on alone. In the summer of 1941 Germany attacked the Soviet Union and had, at first, a series of stunning victories. Then in December the Japanese came in, devastating the American forces at Pearl Harbor and sweeping throughout Asia.

Leacock lived to see the turn of the tide in 1943, but his health was failing fast. He had had an operation for prostate cancer in 1938 and now, it appeared, he had cancer of the throat. He found it increasingly difficult to swallow and to speak. Leacock faced his fate bravely. In a 1940 essay, "Three Score and Ten," he had written that old age was like going over the top from the trenches toward eternity. The mist gathers ahead and the tumult from behind dies down. One by one, the comrades drop away. "Can you hear me? Call to me. I am alone. This must be the end." In 1944 he went into hospital for what he probably knew was a futile operation. He set his affairs in order and wrote a last letter to Fitz. "I have good hopes & I am sure that you have."

According to Stevie, his father knew that his time was up. "Give me my stick," Leacock had written in "Three Score and Ten," "I'm going out on to No Man's Land. I'll face it." He had an operation in Montreal that did not succeed. He was then moved to a hospital in Toronto, where he had a second one. He died there on March 28. His last words were said to have been to his radiologist: "Did I behave pretty well? Was I a good boy?" Leacock's death was regarded as a national loss and made international news. *The New York Herald Tribune* wrote, "Stephen Leacock, surely, was the First Citizen of Canada."

# CHAPTER TEN

# Why Leacock Matters

One day, if you are near Orillia and have some time, take a trip to Stephen Leacock's house on Old Brewery Bay. Ignore the signs for Casino Rama with its 2,500 slot machines and 110 gaming tables which are open 24 hours a day and follow a small road toward Lake Couchiching. You will pass factories and subdivisions and then suddenly, there is the lake, stretching out into the distance. Leacock's house is now a museum, but it has changed very little from when he spent his summers there. The gardens still slope toward the water and the boathouse. The house is still filled with his furniture; even his old gardening hats still hang on pegs beside the door. His books are everywhere, evidence of his voracious reading on every subject under the sun. The house and the place will remind you of an earlier Canada, still a very English one, but the books will remind you that here lived a man with a restless and inquiring mind.

He lived through great changes in Canada and in the world, and his writings are part of the record we have of the past. As a public intellectual and commentator, he helped to define and debate the great questions facing his own time. This is not just of historical interest. Many of the issues he dealt with, whether humorously or seriously (and often he did both at once), are still important to us today. How do we build a fair society? Harness the creativity and vitality of capitalism without stifling it, yet regulate it so that it does not shake itself to smithereens? What is education *for?* And for Canadians, he asked, as we still do today, who are we? And where are we going?

Leacock's story is bound up in that of Canada. He was young when this country was young too. They grew to maturity together. He lived to see a part of the British Empire become, step by peaceful step, an independent country. He saw Great Britain fade as a world power and Canada gravitating toward its increasingly powerful neighbour to the south. He witnessed the development of a Canadian identity, partly coloured by the huge land itself and its stern climate, partly shaped by a shared pride in the achievements of Canadians and their shared sorrows in war and the Depression. Leacock played his part in creating that identity, by writing about Canada and its history, but most importantly by making Canadians and the wider world realize that we were interesting and, yes, funny.

His history is dull, for all the occasional marvellous passage, and his economics and politics have not stood the test of time. Indeed even in their own time they were often written off as lightweight or shallow. "I don't think," said Eugene Forsey, "he ever produced the kind of serious work that he was evidently capable of doing." Leacock was so bright that he could coast in neutral, without fully engaging his brain. He is remembered today for his humour and that is as it should be. "There is not yet a Canadian literature," Leacock wrote in 1941. "Nor is there similarly a Canadian humour, nor any particularly Canadian way of being funny." How wrong he was of course. He was in the middle of creating both.

## SOURCES

### Books, Selected Pamphlets, and Lectures by Stephen Leacock

Cited in order of publication. The first Canadian edition or issue is cited unless there was no Canadian edition in the year of first publication, in which case the first American edition or the first British edition is cited.

Leacock, Stephen. *Elements of Political Science* (New York: Houghton, Mifflin and Company, 1906).

———. *Greater Canada: An Appeal: Let Us No Longer Be a Colony* (Montreal: The Montreal News Company, 1907).

———. *Baldwin, Lafontaine, Hincks: Responsible Government* (Toronto: Morang & Co., 1907).

———. *Literary Lapses: A Book of Sketches* (Montreal: Gazette Printing Company, 1910).

———. *Nonsense Novels* (Montreal: Publishers' Press, 1911).

———. *Sunshine Sketches of a Little Town* (Toronto: Bell and Cockburn, 1912).

———. *Behind the Beyond, and Other Contributions to Human Knowledge* (Toronto: Bell and Cockburn, 1913).

———. *Arcadian Adventures with the Idle Rich* (Toronto: Bell and Cockburn, 1914).

——. *The Dawn of Canadian History: A Chronicle of Aboriginal Canada and the Coming of the White Man* (Toronto: Glasgow, Brook & Company, 1914).

——. *The Mariner of St. Malo: A Chronicle of the Voyages of Jacques Cartier* (Toronto: Glasgow, Brook & Company, 1914).

——. *Adventurers of the Far North* (Toronto: Glasgow, Brook & Company, 1914).

——. *Moonbeams from the Larger Lunacy* (Toronto: S.B. Gundy, 1915).

——. *Essays and Literary Studies* (Toronto: S.B. Gundy, 1916).

——. *Further Foolishness: Sketches and Satires on the Follies of the Day* (Toronto: S.B. Gundy, 1916).

——. *Frenzied Fiction* (Toronto: S.B. Gundy, 1917).

——. *The Hohenzollerns in America, with the Bolsheviks in Berlin, and Other Impossibilities* (Toronto: S.B. Gundy, 1919).

——. *The Unsolved Riddle of Social Justice* (Toronto: S.B. Gundy, 1920).

——. *Winsome Winnie, and Other New Nonsense Novels* (Toronto: S.B. Gundy, 1920).

——. *My Discovery of England* (Toronto: S.B. Gundy, 1922).

——. *Over the Footlights* (Toronto: S.B. Gundy, 1923).

——. *College Days* (Toronto: S.B. Gundy, 1923).

——. *The Garden of Folly* (Toronto: S.B. Gundy, 1924).

——. *Winnowed Wisdom* (Toronto: The Macmillan Company of Canada, 1926).

——. *Short Circuits* (Toronto: The Macmillan Company of Canada, 1928).

——. *The Iron Man and the Tin Woman, with Other Such Futurities: A Book of Little Sketches of To-day and To-morrow* (Toronto: The Macmillan Company of Canada, 1929).

——. *Economic Prosperity in the British Empire* (Toronto: The Macmillan Company of Canada, 1930).

——. *Laugh with Leacock: An Anthology of the Best Work of Stephen Leacock* (New York: Dodd, Mead & Company, 1930).

——. *Wet Wit and Dry Humour: Distilled from the Pages of Stephen Leacock* (New York: Dodd, Mead & Company, 1931).

——. *Back to Prosperity: The Great Opportunity of the Empire Conference* (Toronto: The Macmillan Company of Canada, 1932).

——. *The Dry Pickwick, and Other Incongruities* (London: The Bodley Head, 1932).

——. *Afternoons in Utopia* (Toronto: The Macmillan Company of Canada, 1932).

——. *Mark Twain.* (London: Peter Davies, 1932).

——. *Stephen Leacock's Plan to Relieve the Depression in 6 Days, To Remove It in 6 Months, To Eradicate It in 6 Years* (Toronto: The Macmillan Company of Canada, 1933).

——. *Charles Dickens: His Life and Work* (London: Peter Davies, 1933).

——. *Lincoln Frees the Slaves* (New York: G.P. Putnam's Sons, 1934).

——. *The Greatest Pages of Charles Dickens* (Garden City, NY: Doubleday Doran, 1934).

——. *The Pursuit of Knowledge: A Discussion of Freedom and Compulsion in Education.* Kappa Delta Pi Lecture Series (New York: Liveright Publishing, 1934).

——. *Humour: Its Theory and Technique: With Examples and Samples* (Toronto: Dodd, Mead & Company, 1935).

——. *The Greatest Pages of American Humor: A Study of the Rise and Development of Humorous Writings in America with Selections from the Most Notable of the Humorists* (Garden City, NY: Doubleday Doran, 1936).

——. *Hellements of Hickonomics, in Hiccoughs of Verse Done in Our Social Planning Mill* (New York: Dodd, Mead & Company, 1936).

——. *Funny Pieces: A Book of Random Sketches* (New York: Dodd, Mead & Company, 1936).

——. *My Discovery of the West: A Discussion of East and West in Canada* (Toronto: Thomas Allen, 1937).

——. *Here Are My Lectures and Stories* (New York: Dodd, Mead & Company, 1937).

——. *Humour and Humanity: An Introduction of the Study of Humour* (London: Thornton Butterworth, 1937).

——. *Model Memoirs, and Other Sketches from Simple to Serious* (New York: Dodd, Mead & Company, 1938).

——. *Too Much College, or Education Eating Up Life: With Kindred Essays in Education and Humour* (New York: Dodd, Mead & Company, 1939).

——. *The British Empire: Its Structure, Its Unity, Its Strength* (New York: Dodd, Mead & Company, 1940).

——. *Canada: The Foundations of Its Future* (Montreal: House of Seagram, 1941).

——. *My Remarkable Uncle, and Other Sketches* (New York: Dodd, Mead & Company, 1942).

——. *Our Heritage of Liberty: Its Origin, Its Achievement, Its Crisis: A Book for War Time* (London: The Bodley Head, 1942).

——. *Montreal: Seaport and City* (Garden City, NY: Doubleday Doran, 1942).

——. *How to Write* (New York: Dodd, Mead & Company, 1943).

——. *Happy Stories, Just to Laugh At* (New York: Dodd, Mead & Company, 1943).

——. *While There Is Time: The Case Against Social Catastrophe* (Toronto: McClelland & Stewart, 1945).

——. *Last Leaves* (Toronto: McClelland & Stewart, 1945).

——. *The Boy I Left Behind Me* (Garden City, NY: Doubleday, 1946).

——. *My Recollection of Chicago and the Doctrine of* Laissez Faire. Edited and introduced by Carl Spadoni. (Toronto: University of Toronto Press, 1998).

## Other Sources

Anderson, Allan. *Remembering Leacock: An Oral History* (Ottawa: Deneau, 1983).

Atwood, Margaret. *Survival: A Thematic Guide to Canadian Literature* (Toronto: McClelland & Stewart, 2004).

Benchley, Robert. "Why Do We Laugh—or Do We?" In *Benchley—Or Else* (New York: Harper, 1947).

Berger, Carl. "The Other Mr. Leacock," *Canadian Literature* 55 (Winter 1973): 23–40.

——. *The Sense of Power: Studies in the Ideas of Canadian Imperialism, 1867–1914* (Toronto: University of Toronto Press, 1971).

——. *The Writing of Canadian History: Aspects of English-Canadian Historical Writing Since 1900*, 2nd ed. (Toronto: University of Toronto Press, 1987).

Bothwell, Robert, Ian Drummond and John English. *Canada, 1900–1945* (Toronto: University of Toronto Press, 1987).

——. *The Penguin History of Canada* (Toronto: Penguin Canada, 2006).

Bowker, Alan. *The Social Criticism of Stephen Leacock*. With an introduction by Bowker. (Toronto: University of Toronto Press, 1973).

——. "Stephen Leacock's Discovery of the West" in *Zeitschrift für Kanada-Studien*, 2002, 22. Jahrgang Nr. 1-2; Band 41, pp. 43–51.

——. *On the Front Line of Life: Stephen Leacock: Memories and Reflections, 1935–1944*. With an introduction by Bowker (Toronto: Dundurn, 2004).

Cameron, Silver Donald. *Faces of Leacock: An Appreciation* (Toronto: Ryerson Press, 1967).

Collard, Edgar Andrew. *The McGill You Knew: An Anthology of Memories, 1920–1960* (Don Mills, ON: Longman Canada, 1975).

Colombo, John Robert. *The Stephen Leacock Quote Book* (Toronto: Colombo, 1996).

Cook, Ramsay. "Stephen Leacock and the Age of Plutocracy, 1902–1921," in *Character and Circumstance: Essays in Honour of Donald Grant Creighton*, ed. John S. Moir (Toronto: Macmillan, 1970).

Curry, Ralph. "Leacock & Benchley: An Acknowledged Literary Debt." *The American Book Collector* 7, no. 7 (March 1957): 11–15.

——. *Stephen Leacock: Humorist and Humanist* (Garden City, NY: Doubleday, 1959). Reprinted with various addenda, an afterword, and an appreciation. Shelburne, ON: Battered Silicon Dispatch Box, 2005.

Davies, Robertson. *Feast of Stephen*. With an introduction by Davies (Toronto: McClelland & Stewart, 1970).

——. *The Penguin Stephen Leacock*. With an introduction by Davies (Toronto: Penguin, 1981).

Doyle, James. *Stephen Leacock: The Sage of Orillia* (Toronto: ECW Press, 1992).

Ferguson, Will. *The Penguin Anthology of Canadian Humour* (Toronto: Viking Canada, 2006).

Frost, Stanley Brice. *McGill University: For the Advancement of Learning* (Montreal: McGill-Queen's University Press, 1984).

Horn, Michiel. "Academics and Canadian Social and Economic Policy in the Depression and War Years," *Journal of Canadian Studies* 13 (1978–9).

Kimball, Elizabeth. *The Man in the Panama Hat: Reminiscences of My Uncle, Stephen Leacock* (Toronto: McClelland & Stewart, 1970).

Legate, David. *Stephen Leacock: A Biography* (Toronto: Macmillan of Canada, 1978).

Lynch, Gerald. *Stephen Leacock: Humour and Humanity* (Kingston, ON: McGill-Queen's University Press, 1988).

McArthur, Peter. *Stephen Leacock*. Biography, critical appreciation, and anthology (Toronto: Ryerson Press, 1923).

Moritz, Albert, and Theresa Moritz. Interview by Liron Taub. University of Toronto. August 5, 2008.

——. *Stephen Leacock: His Remarkable Life* (Markham, ON: Fitzhenry and Whiteside, 2002).

Owram, Douglas. *The Government Generation: Canadian Intellectuals and the State, 1900–1945* (Toronto: University of Toronto Press, 1986).

Spadoni, Carl. *An e-Bibliography of Stephen Leacock* (Shelburne, ON: The Battered Silicon Dispatch Box, 2004).

Staines, David, ed. *Stephen Leacock: A Reappraisal* (Ottawa: University of Ottawa Press, 1986).

——. *The Letters of Stephen Leacock* (Don Mills, ON: Oxford University Press, 2006).

Vanderburgh, George A. *The Writings of Stephen Leacock* (Shelburne, ON: The Battered Silicon Dispatch Box, 2006).

## ACKNOWLEDGMENTS

A number of people have helped to make this book possible. Aubrey and Nancy Russell, John Evans, and the late E. Margaret Baillie told me some marvellous stories about the Leacock they knew and about his family. I have also been fortunate to have received much help from the leading experts on Stephen Leacock. I owe a particular thanks to George Vanderburgh, who lent me his comprehensive and unique collection of Leacock's humorous writings. I am also very grateful to Albert and Theresa Moritz, whose biography of Leacock is the standard work, for their insights and advice; to Alan Bowker, who has written so perceptively on Leacock's social and political views, for discussing them with me and letting me see an unpublished paper on *Sunshine Sketches;* and to David Staines, the meticulous editor of Leacock's letters, for helping me to understand Leacock the man. They have all patiently and generously shared their views with me and corrected my mistakes. If any of the latter remain, I am the only person to blame. John Ralston Saul, the series editor, and Diane Turbide, the editorial director at Penguin, and all the very nice and efficient people at Penguin made helpful suggestions and rightly asked pointed questions. As always, Michael Levine, my agent, was enthusiastic and encouraging. Finally I must thank my wonderful research assistant, Liron Taub, who should more properly be called my collaborator. Not only was he indefatigable in finding material, but he offered perceptive and thoughtful comments from which the final product has benefited immensely.

Note: I have listed only Leacock's most famous publications. For a full listing, please refer to Sources.

1869  Stephen Butler Leacock is born December 30 to Peter and Agnes Leacock in Swanmore, Hampshire, England.

1876  The Leacocks move to a farm near Lake Simcoe, Ontario.

1878  E.P. "Remarkable Uncle" Leacock visits the Leacock farmstead.

1882  Stephen Leacock enrols in Upper Canada College, Toronto.

1887  He graduates from Upper Canada College as head boy. Peter Leacock leaves his wife and children permanently. Stephen enrols in modern languages at the University of Toronto.

1888  Obliged to leave the University of Toronto for financial reasons, Leacock obtains high-school teaching certification from Strathroy Collegiate.

1889  He begins teaching at Uxbridge High School, is offered and takes a job at Upper Canada College; returns to the University of Toronto.

1891   He obtains a bachelor's degree from the University of Toronto.

1894   Leacock's first humorous sketch is published.

1895   "My Financial Career" is published in *Life*.

1899   Leacock enrols in the University of Chicago to study political economy.

1900   He marries Beatrix Hamilton.

1901   Leacock obtains a lectureship at McGill University.

1903   He obtains a Ph.D. from the University of Chicago.

1906   *Elements of Political Science* is published.

1907   Leacock lectures internationally on imperial unity for the Cecil Rhodes Trust.

1908   He purchases land to build Old Brewery Bay in Orillia, Ontario, and is appointed head of the Department of Political Economy at McGill.

1910   *Literary Lapses* is published.

1911   *Nonsense Novels* is published.

1912   *Sunshine Sketches of a Little Town* is published.

1914   *Arcadian Adventures with the Idle Rich* is published.

1914–18   World War One

1915      Stephen Lushington Leacock is born August 19.

1919      *The Unsolved Riddle of Social Justice* is published.

1921      Leacock begins his lecture tour through Britain.

1925      Beatrix Leacock falls ill and dies of cancer.

1928      Leacock builds a new house at Old Brewery Bay.

1929      The Great Depression starts.

1930      *Economic Prosperity in the British Empire* is published.

1934      Agnes Leacock dies.

1936      Leacock is forced to retire from McGill; undertakes lecture tour of western Canada.

1937      *My Discovery of the West* wins the Governor General's Literary Award.

1939–45   World War Two

1944      Leacock dies of cancer March 28.

1946      *The Boy I Left Behind Me* is published.